UNITED IN CHRIST

Preparing the Liturgy of the Word at Catholic Weddings

Leisa Anslinger

Jennifer Kerr Breedlove

Charles A. Bobertz

Mary A. Ehle

Christopher J. Ferraro

Mary G. Fox

Corinna Laughlin

Biagio Mazza

LITURGY
TRAINING
PUBLICATIONS

Nihil Obstat
Very Reverend Daniel A. Smilanic, JCD
Vicar for Canonical Services
Archdiocese of Chicago
March 21, 2016

Imprimatur
Very Reverend Ronald A. Hicks
Vicar General
Archdiocese of Chicago
March 21, 2016

UNITED IN CHRIST: PREPARING THE LITURGY OF THE WORD AT CATHOLIC WEDDINGS © 2016 Archdiocese of Chicago: Liturgy Training Publications, 3949 South Racine Avenue, Chicago, IL 60609; 1-800-933-1800; fax 1-800-933-7094; e-mail: orders@ltp.org; website: www.LTP.org. All rights reserved.

This book was edited by Danielle A. Noe, MDIV. Christopher Magnus was the production editor. Kari Nicholls was the designer and the production artist.

The cover image: The Crosiers/Gene Plaisted, OSC. The stained glass window depicting the wedding feast at Cana is found in Nativity Church, Bloomington, Minnesota.

Printed in the United States of America.

20 19 18 17 16   1 2 3 4 5

Library of Congress Control Number: 2016937283

ISBN 978-1-61671-239-6

UIC

Preparing Your Catholic Wedding

Congratulations on your engagement! *United in Christ* has been written for couples like yourself, who have chosen to celebrate Marriage in the Catholic Church. As with many aspects of the day of your wedding, there are choices to be made, including the selection of readings and certain prayers for your ceremony. The Church encourages you to make these choices together.

The Liturgy of the Word at Catholic Weddings

Like all Catholic services, the wedding ceremony, whether within Mass or outside of Mass, always includes a Liturgy of the Word, the set order of readings from Scripture. The readings for weddings express our belief in a loving God. The Liturgy of the Word at a Catholic wedding usually follows the same order as at Sunday Mass.* The Scripture readings the Church provides as options for wedding ceremonies are included in this resource:

The Celebration of Matrimony

In addition to the readings from Scripture, the Church encourages couples to select a few prayers for the Celebration of Matrimony itself (which takes place after the readings and the homily). These prayers and texts are provided in this resource:

Using United in Christ

United in Christ has been prepared to help you choose the readings and certain texts for your wedding ceremony. This task is probably new to you—and that's ok! The features in this book will help make this an easy and prayerful process so that your ceremony will have special meaning for you on your wedding day and throughout your married life. This book will guide you through thoughtful reflection together so that each reading and prayer may reflect what you hold in your hearts as you begin your life together in the presence of God and the people who will gather to celebrate with you.

This book includes:

- background information and reflections on each of the readings so that you can select texts that reflect your love and belief in God;

- an at-a-glance reference noting the reasons why you might select a particular reading, helping you to connect it to your everyday experiences and all you hope for as you begin married life;

- suggestions for readings that fit well together;

- the options for the consent (vows), blessing and giving of rings, and the Nuptial Blessing;

- sample Prayer of the Faithful with tips to help you write your own prayers;

- a form for you to complete indicating to your presider which readings and prayers you have chosen. It is found on **page 92**. It is also available as an edtible PDF. You may access it here: www.ltp.org/UIC_selection_form.

May your wedding celebration be an expression of the love and hope of this special day, a reflection of the love of God to whom you entrust your lives together.

---

* In some cases, it is advised that couples omit one of the readings. The presider or person assisting you with Marriage preparation will let you know if it is appropriate for you to have a shorter Liturgy of the Word. A shorter Liturgy of the Word includes one reading (Old or New Testament) followed by the Responsorial Psalm, Acclamation before the Gospel, and the Gospel reading.

** During Easter Time, the First Reading should be from the New Testament Book of Revelation (**page 56**, see **NT–14**).

The Old Testament Readings

*The First Reading at a Catholic wedding is usually drawn from one of the books of the Old Testament (during Easter Time the First Reading should be from the New Testament Book of Revelation, see **page 56, NT–14**). In this chapter, you will find eight different options for readings from the Old Testament. These options are numbered as **OT–1, OT–2**, and so on. Each reading is followed by a reflection which provides background on the Scripture passage as well as thoughts about what the reading has to say about Marriage.*

Some of the options from the Old Testament will sound very familiar—for example, the creation of human beings from the Book of Genesis. There are other Scripture passages you may not have encountered before.

*You will need to select just one reading from the eight Old Testament readings included in this section. One reading for your wedding liturgy must be about Marriage. These readings have been marked with an asterisk. Read each passage prayerfully together and talk about it. Take your time—don't feel you must choose all the readings for your wedding in one sitting. Spend time talking about each passage, and discuss the commentary that is provided as well. What resonates with you? Which of these readings speaks most directly not just to one of you, but to the relationship you have formed together? You will notice some readings have a long form and a short form to choose from. The short form is in brackets. Record your First Reading selection on the form on **page 92** and give it to your priest or deacon.*

OT-1 *Male and female he created them.*

A reading from the Book of Genesis   *1:26–28, 31a**

Then God said:
"Let us make man in our image, after our likeness.
Let them have dominion over the fish of the sea,
    the birds of the air, and the cattle,
    and over all the wild animals
    and all the creatures that crawl on the ground."

God created man in his image;
    in the image of God he created him;
    male and female he created them.

God blessed them, saying:
    "Be fertile and multiply;
    fill the earth and subdue it.
Have dominion over the fish of the sea,
        the birds of the air,
    and all the living things that move on the earth."
God looked at everything he had made, and he found it very good.

The word of the Lord.

You might select this reading because . . .
You seek to care for the earth by the way you live, not giving in to excesses of
material goods. • As a couple, you are interested in bird watching and are mindful
of the needs of God's creatures. • Your relationship has grown through gardening,
farming, or membership in an environmental organization.

If you select this reading, you might also consider . . .
Psalm 148:1–2, 3–4, 9–10, 11–13a, 13c–14a **(RP–7)** • Revelation 19:1, 5–9a
(NT–14) • Matthew 7:21, 24–29 **(G–3)**

Background of the Reading

Genesis' first creation story recounting the creation of the world in six days with God resting on the seventh conveys significant insights about human nature and relationships. God creates "man," meaning humanity, on the last day, signifying that humanity is the pinnacle and summit of all God's creation. Humanity is created both male and female in God's image and likeness, signifying that humans are both distinct yet complementary, as well as charged with the responsibility of being God's representatives on earth. God's first commandment to human beings is to "be fertile and multiply" asserting that humans take an active part in God's creative activity thus assuring the continuance of humanity.

In giving humanity dominion over all of God's creation, humans are mandated not to abuse creation for their own purposes but to care for all of creation in the same manner that God would. The passage ends with God observing the beauty and wonder of all creation and affirming all of it as "very good," with human beings as the best creative work that God has done. Never forget that all God has created is good.

This creation account is not meant to be taken literally. Rather it asserts the faith stance of the community that produced it, affirming many of their beliefs in a loving God who creates out of love and shares that love with all creation, most especially human beings. As people of faith about to enter into a lifelong covenant commitment with each other, you too affirm these key beliefs about our God, about our role in God's creation, and our responsibility to care for all creation in God's name.

In choosing this passage, you too are asserting the wonders of God's creative love that you will share in a most intimate manner when you are united as one. Created in love and in God's image and likeness, you also will create in love and share that same image and likeness with which you have been gifted with others. You are both God's representatives on earth, and in committing yourselves to one another before God, you commit yourselves to living as God desires. You promise to care lovingly for children, for the earth, and for all living creatures, sensitive to their needs, attentive to the environment, and committed to establishing harmony with all creation. No matter how overwhelming life may become, remain faithful to one another and to God as God does to you.

OT-2 *The two of them become one body.*

A reading from the Book of Genesis   *2:18–24**

The LORD God said: "It is not good for the man to be alone.
I will make a suitable partner for him."
So the LORD God formed out of the ground
    various wild animals and various birds of the air,
    and he brought them to the man to see what he would call them;
    whatever the man called each of them would be its name.
The man gave names to all the cattle,
    all the birds of the air, and all wild animals;
    but none proved to be the suitable partner for the man.

So the LORD God cast a deep sleep on the man,
    and while he was asleep,
    he took out one of his ribs and closed up its place with flesh.
The LORD God then built up into a woman the rib
    that he had taken from the man.
When he brought her to the man, the man said:

    "This one, at last, is bone of my bones
        and flesh of my flesh;
    This one shall be called 'woman,'
        for out of 'her man' this one has been taken."

That is why a man leaves his father and mother
    and clings to his wife,
    and the two of them become one body.

The word of the Lord.

You might select this reading because . . .
You look on Marriage as a partnership that unites a couple in Christ. • Your
relationship is such that you see the goodness that your spouse-to-be brings to
the Marriage. • As a couple, you have worked through issues as partners.

If you select this reading, you might also consider . . .
Psalm 34:2–3, 4–5, 6–7, 8–9 (**RP–2**) • Ephesians 5:2a, 21–33 (**NT–7**) •
Mark 10:6–9 (**G–6**)

Background of the Reading

Ancient authors often used stories about the past in order to explain present reality. Never intended to be taken literally, these stories were a means of explaining the origins of present reality and experience. The reality that the author attempts to explain by this story deals with why men and women are sexually attracted to each other and eventually marry. The passage begins with God becoming aware of the fact that it is not good for a human being to be alone. The author's rich theological position is that just like God, we are wired for community and for social engagement.

Humans are created for entering into partnership with each other, each bringing their own unique and gifted self to the relationship. The detail about creating one human being from the rib of the other communicates the reality that unlike the rest of creation, human beings are deeply connected with and dependent on each other. All of creation is interconnected, of course, but none as deeply and as intimately as men and women. Each recognizes the other as equal and as the best and most fitting partner, the one that completes and fulfills the other. That is why the passage ends the way it does. This attraction and desire to be with the other results in each leaving behind their parental connection, and "clinging" to the other such that "the two of them become one body."

In no way can this passage be used to show woman's inferiority and dependence on man. The author sees marriage as a partnership in which both play equal but significantly different roles. To "leave" and to "cling" are words connected with covenant relationship, asserting that marriage is not a contract but a lifelong, enduring, intimate, faithful, and ever-loving covenant relationship. You may experience the pull of friends, culture, and/or society asserting the belief that women are inferior to and dependent on men. That is not the biblical perspective and it should never be operative in the marriage covenant.

In choosing this passage, reflect on how covenant differs greatly from contract. Covenant involves the whole person, with all their uniqueness, specialness, and giftedness, willingly giving of self to the other so that both can become one eternally united in love. With God's gracious help, each puts love of the other above all else. Each helps the other be the best person they can be, no matter what life brings.

OT-3 *In his love for Rebekah, Isaac found solace after the death of his mother.*

A reading from the Book of Genesis   *24:48–51, 58–67**

The servant of Abraham
    said to Laban:
"I bowed down in worship
    to the LORD,
    blessing the LORD, the God of my
    master Abraham,
    who had led me on the right road
    to obtain the daughter of my
    master's kinsman for his son.
If, therefore, you have in mind to
    show true loyalty to my master,
    let me know;
    but if not, let me know that, too.
I can then proceed accordingly."

Laban and his household
    said in reply;
    "This thing comes from the LORD;
    we can say nothing to you either
    for or against it.
Here is Rebekah, ready for you;
    take her with you,
    that she may become the wife
    of your master's son,
    as the LORD has said."

So they called Rebekah and
    asked her,
    "Do you wish to go with this man?"
She answered, "I do."
At this time they allowed their
    sister Rebekah and her nurse
    to take leave,
    along with Abraham's servant
    and his men.
Invoking a blessing on Rebekah,
    they said:

"Sister, may you grow
    into thousands of myriads;
And may your descendants
    gain possession
    of the gates of their enemies!"

Then Rebekah and her maids
    started out;
    they mounted their camels and
    followed the man.
So the servant took Rebekah and went
    on his way.

Meanwhile Isaac had gone from the
    Beer-lahai-roi
    and was living in the region
    of Negeb.
One day toward evening he went
    out . . . in the field,
    and as he looked around,
    he noticed that camels were ap-
    proaching.
Rebekah, too, was looking about, and
    when she saw him,
    she alighted from her camel and
    asked the servant,
    "Who is the man out there,
    walking through the fields
    toward us?"
"That is my master," replied the servant.
Then she covered herself with her veil.

The servant recounted to Isaac all the
    things he had done.
Then Isaac took Rebekah into his tent;
    he married her, and thus she be-
    came his wife.
In his love for her Isaac found solace
    after the death of his mother Sarah.

The word of the Lord.

Background of the Reading

The context for this passage is the approaching death of Abraham and his desire to see his only son Isaac wed the woman God has chosen for him. Abraham commissions his servant to find such a woman for Isaac and having discovered her through her gracious hospitality at a well, the servant now pleads with Laban, Rebekah's brother, to give his permission for her to marry Isaac. While this exemplifies the custom of arranged marriages in a traditional tribal setting, the underlying messages concerning this love relationship should not be minimized.

The passage understands this marriage as guided by God. From a faith perspective, attraction to the other is not just a biological or psychological experience, but is seen as ultimately directed by God's hidden hand and purpose. In asking Rebekah if she was willing to leave her family and go with Abraham's servant, Rebekah, just like Abraham himself, says yes and is willing to take the risk of leaving home and trusting God in the process. Any love relationship will have to pronounce that yes and be willing to take the risk to go where God is guiding you. From a faith perspective, such a journey and commitment anticipates God's blessings on the couple and through them on all others.

As they near the place where Isaac resides, Rebekah spies him out even before she knows who he is. Her inquiry about him indicates her immediate attraction to him. For the author, this is a definite indication that God guides one's choice of the other and intends them to be together. Upon seeing her, Isaac welcomes her into his tent and marries her. Rebekah becomes his wife and partner, and Isaac finds "solace" in her.

As you reflect on your union, reflect on how God has brought you together, guides your paths, and continues to be with you as you journey through life together.

You might select this reading because . . .
You consider that God brought you together. • Your relationship has been nurtured through your parish community. • As a couple, you see that God was at work in the way you met and the path your courtship took.

If you select this reading, you might also consider . . .
Psalm 112:1bc–2, 3–4, 5–7a, 7bc–8, 9 (**RP–4**) • Romans 12:1–2, 9–18 (**NT–2**) • Matthew 5:1–12a (**G–1**)

OT-4 *May the Lord of heaven prosper you both. May he grant you mercy and peace.*

A reading from the Book of Tobit *7:6–14**

Raphael and Tobiah entered the house
of Raguel and greeted him.
Raguel sprang up and kissed Tobiah,
shedding tears of joy.
But when he heard that Tobit had lost
his eyesight,
he was grieved and wept aloud.
He said to Tobiah:
"My child, God bless you!
You are the son of a noble
and good father.
But what a terrible misfortune
that such a righteous and
charitable man
should be afflicted with blindness!"
He continued to weep in the arms
of his kinsman Tobiah.
His wife Edna also wept for Tobit;
and even their daughter Sarah
began to weep.

Afterward, Raguel slaughtered
a ram from the flock
and gave them a cordial reception.
When they had bathed and reclined
to eat,
Tobiah said to Raphael,
"Brother Azariah,
ask Raguel to let me marry my
kinswoman Sarah."
Raguel overheard the words;
so he said to the boy:
"Eat and drink and be
merry tonight,
for no man is more entitled to marry
my daughter Sarah
than you, brother.

Besides, not even I have the right to
give her to anyone but you,
because you are my closest relative.
But I will explain the situation to you
very frankly.
I have given her in marriage to
seven men,
all of whom were kinsmen of ours,
and all died on the very night they
approached her.
But now, son, eat and drink.
I am sure the Lord will look after
you both."
Tobiah answered, "I will eat or
drink nothing
until you set aside what belongs
to me."

Raguel said to him: "I will do it.
She is yours according to the decree
of the Book of Moses.
Your marriage to her has been decided
in heaven!
Take your kinswoman
from now on you are her love,
and she is your beloved.
She is yours today and ever after.
And tonight, son, may the Lord
of heaven prosper you both.
May he grant you mercy and peace."
Then Raguel called his daughter Sarah,
and she came to him.
He took her by the hand and gave her
to Tobiah with the words:
"Take her according to the law.
According to the decree written in the
Book of Moses she is your wife.
Take her and bring her back safely to
your father.

And may the God of heaven
grant both of you peace
and prosperity."
He then called her mother and told
her to bring a scroll,
so that he might draw up a
marriage contract
stating that he gave
Sarah and Tobiah as his wife
according to the decree
of the Mosaic law.
Her mother brought the scroll,
and he drew up the contract,
to which they affixed their seals.

Afterward they began to eat
and drink.

The word of the Lord.

Background of the Reading

This charming tale of marriage, another example of the custom of
arranged marriage in a traditional tribal setting, conveys deep truths
about the risks involved in any love relationship. Tobiah, son of Tobit,
is guided on his journey to procure resources for his blind ailing
father by the angel Raphael, disguised as a distant relative. Raphael,
a messenger and representative of God, guides and assists Tobiah
on the journey and counsels him to marry Sarah.

Tobiah asks Raguel, Sarah's father, for her hand in marriage and
he agrees but first Raguel tells Tobiah of the risks involved, namely
that Sarah's husbands had died at the hands of a demon. Tobiah does
not seem to be deterred by such news and refuses to eat or drink till
Raguel consents to the marriage. Raguel agrees and, with his wife,
draws up a marriage contract according to Mosaic law, giving Sarah
to Tobiah in lawful marriage. Only when the contract is signed
does Tobiah agree to eat and drink, thus sealing the bond between
both families.

Raphael symbolically represents God's role in any marriage.
From a faith perspective, God guides our choice of the other, and
assures us that no matter the risks involved, God will be there to
walk with us as we face the many challenges of life. In choosing
this reading, you affirm this belief and proclaim it to others.

You might select this reading because . . .
You seek and trust God's guidance. • In your relationship, you have relied on God
and feel that he has led you to marry this person. • As a couple, you are drawn to
look for God in whatever path you take.

If you select this reading, you might also consider . . .
Psalm 34:2–3, 4–5, 6–7, 8–9 (RP–2) • 1 Corinthians 12:31—13:8a (NT–5) •
Matthew 5:13–16 (G–2)

OT–5 *Allow us to live together to a happy old age.*

A reading from the Book of Tobit 8:4b–8*

On their wedding night Tobiah arose from bed and
    said to his wife,
      "Sister, get up. Let us pray and beg our Lord
    to have mercy on us and grant us deliverance."
Sarah got up, and they started to pray
    and beg that deliverance might be theirs.
They began with these words:

      "Blessed are you, O God of our fathers;
          praised be your name forever and ever.
      Let the heavens and all your creation
          praise you forever.
      You made Adam and you gave him his wife Eve
          to be his help and support;
          and from these two the human race descended.
      You said, 'It is not good for the man to be alone;
          let us make him a partner like himself.'
      Now, Lord, you know that I take this wife of mine
          not because of lust,
          but for a noble purpose.
      Call down your mercy on me and on her,
          and allow us to live together to a happy old age."

They said together, "Amen, amen."

The word of the Lord.

You might select this reading because . . .
You praise God, no matter if there is joy or adversity in your life. • As a couple,
you feel that your relationship is a partnership brought about through God's love
and mercy. • Your Marriage's foundation is based on the nobility of family and
God's purpose.

If you select this reading, you might also consider . . .
Psalm 148:1–2, 3–4, 9–10, 11–13a, 13c–14a **(RP–7)** • Romans 15:1b–3a,
5–7, 13 **(NT–3)** • John 15:9–12 **(G–8)**

Background of the Reading

In living out our faith, prayer is an essential component. Communication with God keeps us attuned to God's ways and values, helping us to align ourselves with God in the midst of life's joys and its many challenges. Prayer focuses our attention on God and through it we come to know and experience God's presence with us on our life journey. This is especially true for any marriage. Prayer is a powerful bond between the couple that not only guides the marriage but sustains it over the long haul.

This passage from Tobit is the prayer that Tobiah and Sarah pray together on their wedding night. Recall that Tobiah was willing to take the risks involved in marrying Sarah, who is possessed by a demon responsible for the death of her previous seven spouses, and, guided by God through the angel Raphael, becomes a source of healing and strength for both of them.

As the marriage journey begins, Tobiah and Sarah pray together for God's gentle touch, mercy, and deliverance from all that would diminish their love relationship. What an ideal way to begin a marriage. This is what you are doing as you celebrate Marriage within the context of a faith community. Notice that both pray together blessing and praising God for the gifts of life, love, and creation. Reaching back to Adam and Eve as models of ideal marriage, they pray that they might be a source of help and support to each other, along with asking God for the richness of children.

They affirm marriage as a gift from God. God created all humans, especially marriage partners, as equal partners, united through caring and nourishing each other in lifelong, enduring, faithful covenant love. Tobiah and Sarah affirm that marriage is not for the sake of merely satisfying sexual needs, but that sexual attraction for the other has a higher purpose, namely to help each other live in selfless love by giving of oneself completely to the other, and to all those others, especially children, that will enter into their married lives. Their prayer ends by asking for God's care and mercy, and that with God's help they will live together to a "happy old age."

Selecting this passage will help you focus on prayer as an essential component of the lifelong Marriage commitment, along with highlighting the attitudes and perspectives that should be the hallmarks of any good Christian Marriage.

OT-6 *The woman who fears the Lord is to be praised.*

A reading from the Book of Proverbs   *31:10–13, 19–20, 30–31**

When one finds a worthy wife,
    her value is far beyond pearls.
Her husband, entrusting his heart to her,
    has an unfailing prize.
She brings him good, and not evil,
    all the days of her life.
She obtains wool and flax
    and makes cloth with skillful hands.
She puts her hands to the distaff,
    and her fingers ply with the spindle.
She reaches out her hands to the poor,
    and extends her arms to the needy.
Charm is deceptive and beauty fleeting;
    the woman who fears the LORD is to be praised.
Give her a reward of her labors,
    and let her works praise her at the city gates.

The word of the Lord.

You might select this reading because . . .
As a couple, you are grateful to God for bringing you together. • You understand
the depth and integrity that each brings to the Marriage. • Your relationship has
deepened to understand that our faith needs to be the foundation for Marriage.

If you select this reading, you might also consider . . .
Psalm 128:1–2, 3, 4–5ac and 6a **(RP–5)** • Romans 12:1–2, 9–18 **(NT–2)** •
Matthew 5:1–12a **(G–1)**

Background of the Reading

This poem or song from the Book of Proverbs praises the ideal wife. Often marriage songs in Scripture expound upon the physical beauty of the wife. Here, it is not so much the wife's physical beauty that is highlighted but her admirable power and strength both as an individual and as one caring for her household. The patriarchal backdrop to the poem often shies couples away from using this passage, for fear of stereotyping women and reinforcing the superiority of men. However, a deeper understanding of the passage surfaces qualities that are equally applicable to both partners in the marriage relationship.

Proverbs personifies Wisdom as a woman, a gift from God to all persons who seek to know the Lord and walk in God's ways. This Wisdom Woman calls out to us all of our lives, inviting us to learn of her wisdom so as to live full human lives connected to God and one another. The poem in Proverbs of the ideal wife is a direct personification of Wisdom Woman in action, not just as a wife but as a template for all human beings who have incorporated God's wisdom into their daily life. In this manner, the qualities of the ideal wife are applicable across the board to all people attuned to God's wisdom ways. This is especially true in a marriage relationship.

Wisdom people are strong, valiant people whose value is beyond words. As married partners, each entrusts their heart to the other, valuing the other as an "unfailing prize." Each does what is needed to provide for the other and the family, using their special gifts in an industrious and wise manner. Each is called to reach out to the poor and the needy, manifesting God's care for all, especially the weak and vulnerable.

The last two verses summarize well the intent of the whole poem, namely that lifelong loving relationship rests not in physical beauty or external charm but in shared awe, reverence, and respect for the Lord. Life lived from such a perspective will ultimately be rewarded by God and praised by all. The poem expresses well the ideals of married life not just for the wife but for the husband as well. May you always manage your lives with awe and reverence of God while being continually attuned to God's wisdom.

OT–7 *Stern as death is love.*

A reading from the Song of Songs *2:8–10, 14, 16a; 8:6–7a*

Hark! my lover — here he comes
  springing across the mountains,
  leaping across the hills.
My lover is like a gazelle
  or a young stag.
Here he stands behind our wall,
  gazing through the windows,
  peering through the lattices.
My lover speaks; he says to me,
  "Arise, my beloved, my dove, my beautiful one, and come!

"O my dove in the clefts of the rock,
  in the secret recesses of the cliff,
Let me see you,
  let me hear your voice,
For your voice is sweet,
  and you are lovely."

My lover belongs to me and I to him.
  He says to me:

"Set me as a seal on your heart,
  as a seal on your arm;
For stern as death is love,
  relentless as the nether–world is devotion;
  its flames are a blazing fire.
Deep waters cannot quench love,
  nor floods sweep it away."

The word of the Lord.

You might select this reading because . . .
You have experienced adversity in your relationship and found that it did not
diminish your love. • As a couple, you draw strength and vitality from each other. •
Your devotion to each other has been strengthened during your courtship.

If you select this reading, you might also consider . . .
Psalm 103:1–2, 8 and 13, 17–18a **(RP–3)** • Romans 8:31b–35, 37–39 **(NT–1)** •
Matthew 7:21, 24–29 **(G–3)**

Background of the Reading

Song of Songs is a collection of love songs expressing the beauty, power, and strength of love. These love songs speak of yearning for and interacting with the beloved—this leads to intimate union with God. This selection of love songs speaks of the beauty and the power of love which consistently longs to be satisfied.

The seasonal backdrop for these passages is springtime. The woman, confined to her parents' home, sees her lover approaching with swift, graceful, and agile movements like "a gazelle or a young stag." The lover, not able to enter the house, gazes through its windows and lattices as she hears his call to her to come out and be with him. The man pictures his loved one as a dove, a sure sign of spring, hiding in the "secret recesses of the cliff." He implores her to let him see her and hear her voice, for he desires to see her beauty and experience the sweetness of her voice. This passage includes a definite affirmation of intimate love, connection, and union of one with the other, "my lover belongs to me and I to him."

In this reading, the woman asks the man to set her "as a seal on your heart . . . on your arm." A seal, worn either as a necklace that touched the heart or wrapped around one's arm, was used both for identification purposes and for affixing one's signature to something. Such intimate connection seems to be the desire of both lovers.

Love's intense power and strength is then compared to the power that death has over human beings. The strength of both forces is so overwhelming that neither can be avoided and ultimately one simply succumbs. The flames of love are compared to a blazing fire which overpowers all that it touches. Neither deep waters nor floods, the biblical symbols for chaos and disorder, can quench or sweep away love. Love is so powerful that it enables human beings to overcome the challenges and chaos of life.

In choosing this passage, be aware of the beauty and desires that love engenders, while at the same time become deeply aware of the strength and power of love to help both of you face whatever challenges and uncertainty will inevitably surface in your life together.

OT-8 *Like the sun rising in the LORD's heavens, the beauty of a virtuous wife is the radiance of her home.*

A reading from the Book of Sirach   *26:1–4, 13–16**

Blessed the husband of a good wife,
> twice-lengthened are his days;
A worthy wife brings joy to her husband,
> peaceful and full is his life.
A good wife is a generous gift
> bestowed upon him who fears the LORD;
Be he rich or poor, his heart is content,
> and a smile is ever on his face.

A gracious wife delights her husband,
> her thoughtfulness puts flesh on his bones;
A gift from the LORD is her governed speech,
> and her firm virtue is of surpassing worth.
Choicest of blessings is a modest wife,
> priceless her chaste soul.

A holy and decent woman adds grace upon grace;
> indeed, no price is worthy of her temperate soul.
Like the sun rising in the LORD's heavens,
> the beauty of a virtuous wife is the radiance of her home.

The word of the Lord.

You might select this reading because . . .
As a couple, you each realize the importance of valuing and doing special things for each other. • You value generosity of spirit and know that it will nurture a relationship. • Your relationship is dependent upon God, who sends down blessings on each of us.

If you select this reading, you might also consider . . .
Psalm 128:1–2, 3, 4–5ac and 6a **(RP–5)** • Hebrews 13:1–4a, 5–6b **(NT–10)** • John 15:9–12 **(G–8)**

Background of the Reading

Praise of a good wife as a gift from God, with all her attributes and virtues, is a common theme in Biblical literature. The Book of Sirach was written by a wise, older man who is imparting life's learned lessons to young men in his charge. The reading's patriarchal nature is immediately evident in praising a good wife not in her own right but for the blessings and benefits that she provides for her husband, making him happy and content. Because of this perspective, couples shy away from selecting this passage. However, there is need to understand the original perspective first, and then connect it to today's perspective regarding the role of both partners in the marriage covenant.

Our current sensibilities regarding marriage are not from a patriarchal mindset but from a sense of equality between partners who respect the unique gifts that each brings to the marriage. From a patriarchal perspective, the ideal wife is valued for her charm, modesty, silence, chastity, and self-discipline along with her ability to cook and please her husband all at the same time. These qualities would make her husband truly blessed, content, and happy leading to a long life of joy and peace for him. Today, we would have to examine the qualities of a good marriage from the perspectives of both partners, and what each needs to contribute to make the other happy, content, and peaceful, ultimately leading to a long, happy life together.

You enter into a marriage relationship because you value the other for who they are. What matters is the gift of self that you offer to the other, with all of its pluses and minuses. Many of the qualities attributed to a good wife in this reading are qualities that a good husband also needs to cultivate. In so doing, both partners become attuned to the needs of the other, and strive to work together in meeting those needs. Making the other happy, peaceful, and content is a mutual responsibility that each takes on in the marriage commitment.

In selecting this passage, you both realize that each of you commits to adapting oneself to meet the needs of the other, while at the same time remaining the unique and loving person that you are. You form a covenantal partnership that is always alert to not only your own needs, but also the needs of the other.

OT-9 *I will make a new covenant with the house of Israel and the house of Judah.*

A reading from the Book of the Prophet Jeremiah

31:31–32a, 33–34a

The days are coming, says the LORD,
>   when I will make a new covenant with the house of Israel
>   and the house of Judah.
It will not be like the covenant I made with their fathers:
>   the day I took them by the hand
>   to lead them forth from the land of Egypt.
But this is the covenant which I will make
>   with the house of Israel after those days, says the LORD.
I will place my law within them, and write it upon their hearts;
>   I will be their God, and they shall be my people.
No longer will they have need to teach their friends and relatives
>   how to know the LORD.
All, from least to greatest, shall know me, says the LORD.

The word of the Lord.

You might select this reading because . . .
You realize that your Marriage is to model the covenant that God has with us. •
Your faith enables you to draw your spouse-to-be into a relationship that has God
at its foundation. • As a couple, you have learned to rely on God to respond to
each other lovingly during hard times.

If you select this reading, you might also consider . . .
Psalm 33:12 and 18, 20–21, 22 **(RP–1)** • 1 John 3:18–24 **(NT–12)** •
John 15:12–16 **(G–9)**

Background of the Reading

Publically establishing a new covenant with each other is what the marriage ritual is all about. This new covenant differs from any other relationship or covenant that each of you has entered into before. Because of the newness of this covenant relationship and its implications for married life together, the Church offers this passage on God's initiative in establishing a new covenant with Israel as a model or template for the marriage covenant.

The prophet Jeremiah, speaking on God's behalf, offers the suffering and displaced people of God exiled in Babylonia hope and consolation by means of his announcement of a new covenant that God will initiate with Israel. It will be different than the covenant that had been established through Moses on Mt. Sinai on stone tablets, which the Israelite community consistently violated. Rather, this covenant will be written on people's hearts.

The Torah, God's guidance and path for righteous living, calls for the interior conversion of hearts and leads to the faithful and lifelong commitment of the whole person to God, and to service of the other. As a result, all will know the Lord intimately and holistically for their actions will reflect their transformed hearts. This new, internal covenant, different from the previous one, will embrace the entire community equally, with no class or power distinctions. "All, from the least to greatest, shall know me, says the Lord."

In selecting this passage, you recognize God's presence in your Marriage. This empowers each of you with what is needed to follow through on this faithful lifelong commitment. The Marriage covenant, different from any previous covenants, involves your entire self—mind, heart, body—for life. It demands a deep change of mind and heart that is focused on God and each other. This focus, if refined and cultivated, will be apparent in your words and actions toward each other and toward all you encounter.

If you choose this reading, this means that you are willing to go deeper than ever in your relationship with God, each other, and the world. Your faith assures you that God is ever with you, always giving you the power and strength to respond in love to each other and to God. By committing yourself in covenant love, both of you will be transformed with God's help, as you create a new way of relating and living as equal partners committed to knowing and loving the Lord intimately and faithfully.

The Responsorial Psalms

In this section, you will find the seven options for the Responsorial Psalm that is sung at a Catholic wedding liturgy. They are numbered as RP–1, RP–2, and so on. Each psalm is followed by a reflection which provides background on the Scripture passage as well as thoughts about what the psalm has to say about Marriage. One reading for your wedding liturgy must be about Marriage. These readings have been marked with an asterisk.

The Book of Psalms in the Old Testament was, and is, the prayer book of the Jewish people. Jesus grew up learning and praying the psalms. Today, the psalms continue to be the prayer book of the Church. At every wedding, a Responsorial Psalm follows the First Reading (it is called "Responsorial" because it includes a "response," or a refrain, for the congregation to sing). Today, as in ancient times, the psalms are intended to be sung. Usually a cantor sings the verses, alternating with the refrain sung by the entire assembly. Consult with the music director in your parish to discuss musical settings of the Responsorial Psalm to use at your wedding.

Before choosing one psalm, read and reflect on each one. Be sure to consider the refrain which will be sung by you and the entire congregation. Which of these psalms speaks most directly to your aspirations for your Marriage and your relationship with God? Record your psalm selection on the form on **page 92** *and give it to your priest or deacon.*

RP–1 *Psalm 33:12 and 18, 20–21, 22 (5b)*

R. The earth is full of the goodness of the LORD**.**

Blessed the nation whose God
>   is the LORD,
>   the people he has chosen for his
>   own inheritance.
But see, the eyes of the LORD are
>   upon those who fear him,
>   upon those who hope for
>   his kindness. **R.**

Our soul waits for the LORD,
>   who is our help and our shield,
For in him our hearts rejoice;
>   in his holy name we trust. **R.**

May your kindness, O LORD,
>   be upon us
>   who have put our hope in you. **R.**

Background of the Psalm

Weddings are celebrations of abundance and fullness—fullness of
love and joy, a time of being surrounded by friends and family who
love you and celebrate with you. This joyful psalm sings out the praise
of God's goodness and love, proclaiming our trust and rejoicing in
the Lord's steadfast kindness. This is a psalm about intimacy and
connection, and thus it is beautifully appropriate for a wedding
celebration. In it the psalmist sings that God chooses us for his own,
just as Christ chooses the Church, and as a man and woman choose
one another to be joined forever in Marriage. It draws our attention
to the way you, as a couple joining in Matrimony, will stand before
the world as symbols of the way Christ loves all his people. This
covenant relationship between you mirrors the covenant between
God and humanity.

   A couple who chooses this psalm might want to celebrate the way
they and all of us are joined with all creation, drawing attention to
how God's beauty is manifest in the world around them. They might
want to sing a psalm of simple patient trust in a God who always
hears, in whom all their hope rests.

You might select this psalm because . . .
The two of you spend time hiking, camping, or at the beach taking in all that
nature offers. • You are both committed to caring for the earth. • Having
experienced difficult times together, an illness or perhaps the death of a family
member, you have learned as a couple the importance of trusting in the Lord.

If you select this psalm, you might also consider . . .
Genesis 1:26–28, 31a **(OT–1)** • Philippians 4:4–9 **(NT–8)** • John 17:20–26 **(G–10)**

R. I will bless the Lord at all times.

or:

R. Taste and see the goodness of the Lord.

I will bless the LORD at all times;
    his praise shall be ever in
        my mouth.
Let my soul glory in the LORD;
    the lowly will hear me and
        be glad. **R.**

Glorify the LORD with me,
    let us together extol his name.
I sought the LORD, and he
        answered me
and delivered me from all
        my fears. **R.**

Look to him that you may be radiant
        with joy,
    and your faces may not blush
        with shame.
When the poor one called out,
        the LORD heard,
    and from all his distress
        he saved him. **R.**

The angel of the LORD encamps
    around those who fear him,
        and delivers them.
Taste and see how good the LORD is;
    blessed the man who takes
        refuge in him. **R.**

Background of the Psalm

When two people begin their life together, they know that sometimes the journey will be easy and full of joy, while at other times there will be hardship and suffering. This psalm celebrates the goodness of God that will be with you through all of life's challenges. It recognizes that there will be times when in our spiritual or material poverty we will cry out to God, believing in the promise that God will answer. The refrain helps us recognize how close God is to us, in the food we eat and in the sight of everything around us. This psalm of praise and prayer would be a good choice for a couple who wants to acknowledge the challenges that lie ahead, but who also can rejoice in the conviction that God will see them through.

You might select this psalm because . . .
Your trust in God is so deep that, even after one of you lost a job and you needed to postpone the wedding, you found you could praise God. • Life never seemed to taste so sweet as after one of you recovered from an accident.

If you select this psalm, you might also consider . . .
Tobit 7:6–14 (**OT–4**) • Revelation 19:1, 5–9a (**NT–14**) • John 2:1–11 (**G–7**)

RP–3 *Psalm 103:1–2, 8 and 13, 17–18a (8a or cf. 17)*

R. The Lᴏʀᴅ is kind and merciful.
or:
R. The Lᴏʀᴅ's kindness is everlasting to those who fear him.

Bless the Lᴏʀᴅ, O my soul;
  and all my being, bless his
    holy name.
Bless the Lᴏʀᴅ, O my soul,
  and forget not all his benefits. **R.**

Merciful and gracious is the Lᴏʀᴅ,
  slow to anger and abounding
    in kindness.
As a father has compassion on
  his children,

so the Lᴏʀᴅ has compassion on
  those who fear him. **R.**

But the kindness of the Lᴏʀᴅ
  is from eternity
to eternity toward those who
  fear him,
And his justice towards
  children's children
among those who keep
  his covenant. **R.**

Background of the Psalm

The mercy of God is endless, and the kindness of God lasts forever: that is the message of this psalm, with either of its possible responses. The verses of the psalm evoke images of the love in which parents hold their children. This psalm reminds us of how we are loved by our Creator, and it gives example for how we as parents are called to love our children: with kindness and compassion. The final verses remind all of us—and especially you as the new couple—that God's love is not just upon us who gather on your wedding day, but his love will last for generations, blessing your children and your children's children.

The couple who chooses this psalm wants to highlight, on the day of their wedding, the mercy and kindness of God—not just today, but forever, in the lives of their children and grandchildren and all the generations that follow.

You might select this psalm because . . .
As a couple, you view your relationship as a blessing and are thankful that God has united you. • Together you have endured a hardship and look to God with gratitude for help provided. • Your meeting was an unlikely one, and you are appreciative that God allowed you to meet.

If you select this psalm, you might also consider . . .
Jeremiah 31:31–32a, 33–34a (**OT–9**) • Hebrews 13:1–4a, 5–6b (**NT–10**) • Matthew 5:1–12a (**G–1**)

R. Blessed the man who greatly delights in the Lord's commands.

or:

R. Alleluia.

Blessed the man who fears the LORD,
who greatly delights in
his commands.
His posterity shall be mighty upon
the earth;
the upright generation shall
be blessed. **R.**

Wealth and riches shall be in his house;
his generosity shall endure forever.
Light shines through the darkness for
the upright;
he is gracious and merciful
and just. **R.**

Well for the man who is gracious
and lends,
who conducts his affairs with justice;
He shall never be moved;
the just one shall be in everlasting
remembrance.
An evil report he shall not fear. **R.**

His heart is firm, trusting in the LORD.
His heart is steadfast; he shall not fear
till he looks down upon his foes. **R.**

Lavishly he gives to the poor;
his generosity shall endure forever;
his horn shall be exalted in glory. **R.**

Background of the Psalm

Psalm 112 is a song of faith and constancy, of the blessing and peace found by those whose lives follow the path of God. The verses speak of those who live under God's guidance, and the legacy of light and joy this kind of life brings. Notice that the actions of the blessed ones are not rooted in the extraordinary—on the contrary, this psalm speaks of those who live in justice and light, and who are mindful of the poor in their midst.

The couple that chooses this psalm is likely to embrace the call of the Church to give freely to those in need, consciously conducting their lives under the Word and law of the Lord.

You might select this psalm because . . .
You met when both of you took time off work to volunteer in the Peace Corps, AmeriCorps, or a religious lay volunteer ministry. • As a couple, you set aside time to work at a food pantry or soup kitchen. • Your commitment to social justice issues deepened your relationship.

If you select this psalm, you might also consider . . .
Proverbs 31:10–13, 19–20, 30–31 (**OT–6**) • Colossians 3:12–17 (**NT–9**) • Matthew 5:13–16 (**G–2**)

RP–5 *Psalm 128:1–2, 3, 4–5ac and 6a (cf. 1 or 4)**

R. Blessed are those who fear the Lord.

or:

R. See how the Lord blesses those who fear him.

Blessed are you who fear the LORD,
who walk in his ways!
For you shall eat the fruit of
your handiwork;
blessed shall you be,
and favored. **R.**

Your wife shall be like a fruitful vine
in the recesses of your home;

Your children like olive plants
around your table. **R.**

Behold, thus is the man blessed
who fears the LORD.
The LORD bless you from Zion:
may you see the prosperity
of Jerusalem
all the days of your life. **R.**

Background of the Psalm

Psalm 128 is a song of praise and gratitude, and it sings of the blessings that await those who follow and love God, the giver of every good gift. It is also one of the most often used psalms for weddings. It presents to the gathered assembly a vision of the happy and prosperous life that can be found by those who follow God's ways. There are many beautiful musical settings of this psalm, which speaks of the family gathered around the table, fertility and fruitfulness, children flourishing "like olive plants," and images of a life well lived, hard working and prosperous.

Couples who choose this psalm would likely be those who look forward to a happy and simple life, eager to begin a life of fruitful labor, following in the pathways of the Lord, and seeking the blessings of God all their days.

You might select this psalm because . . .
You place your trust in God and value him more than material goods. •
As a couple, you look forward to the riches family life will provide. •
Your family life is a top priority.

If you select this psalm, you might also consider . . .
Sirach 26:1–4, 13–16 (OT–8) • Romans 15:1b–3a, 5–7, 13 (NT–3) •
John 2:1–11 (G–7)

RP–6 *Psalm 145:8–9, 10 and 15, 17–18 (9a)*

R. The Lord is compassionate toward all his works.

The LORD is gracious and merciful,
 slow to anger and of great
  kindness.
The LORD is good to all
 and compassionate toward
  all his works. **R.**

Let all your works give you thanks,
 O LORD,
 and let your faithful ones
  bless you.

The eyes of all look hopefully to you
 and you give them their food in
  due season. **R.**

The LORD is just in all his ways
 and holy in all his works.
The LORD is near to all who call
 upon him,
 to all who call upon him
  in truth. **R.**

Background of the Psalm

Psalm 145 is one of the most familiar and best-loved psalms that the Church sings at various liturgies, from Sunday Mass to special celebrations like weddings. It is a song of gratitude, hope, and praise. It expresses gratitude for the many gifts of God, crying out, "Let all your works give you thanks, O LORD, / and let your faithful ones bless you." The psalmist praises the faithfulness and steadfastness of God's love, affirms that "the LORD is near to all who call," and accepts the call of the faithful to *be* God's works in the world.

The couple who chooses this psalm might be one whose spirituality focuses on their awareness of themselves as both creations of God and also his hands and feet on the earth; they will celebrate God's nearness to them. In the gift of his compassion and kindness to them, they will seek to be kind and compassionate to others, trusting in God to guide and shape their life's journey.

You might select this psalm because . . .
One of you cares for others as their profession, such as the medical profession, social work, or ministry. • You are careful how you treat others and recognize that small kindnesses make a difference to people. • You are known for listening to others' problems compassionately.

If you select this psalm, you might also consider . . .
Tobit 8:4b–8 (**OT–5**) • Romans 12:1–2, 9–13 (**NT–2**) • John 2:1–11 (**G–7**)

R. Let all praise the name of the Lord.

or:

R. Alleluia.

Alleluia.
Praise the LORD from the heavens,
　　praise him in the heights;
Praise him, all you his angels,
　　praise him, all you his hosts. **R.**

Praise him, sun and moon;
　　praise him, all you shining stars.
Praise him, you highest heavens,
　　and you waters above
　　　　the heavens. **R.**

You mountains and you hills,
　　you fruit trees and all you cedars;

You wild beasts and all tame animals,
　　you creeping things and winged
　　　　fowl. **R.**

Let the kings of the earth and all
　　　　peoples,
　　the princes and all the judges
　　　　of the earth,
Young men too, and maidens,
　　old men and boys,
Praise the name of the LORD,
　　for his name alone is exalted. **R.**

His majesty is above earth
　　　　and heaven,
　　and he has lifted his horn above
　　　　the people. **R.**

Background of the Psalm

Is there any time more appropriate for exultant praise than a wedding, or any moment when the joy in God's presence in our lives is more abundant and overflowing? Psalm 148 calls out to all of creation, from the highest to the lowest, to sing praise to God with full heart and voice. Angels, moon, stars, clouds, mountains, trees, animals— all are part of the great song of praise. All of humanity, too, is called to this expansive joy—from the highest of kings to the smallest children, all people of every age.

A couple who wishes to highlight an awareness of the inter-connectedness of all beings on the earth, and to humbly accept humanity's place in the great web of creation, might select this psalm for their wedding.

You might select this psalm because . . .
You feel close to nature and are prone to stay up late counting the stars. •
As a couple, you have volunteered at a shelter for animals. • St. Francis is your favorite saint because of his love and care for animals and creation.

If you select this psalm, you might also consider . . .
Genesis 1:26–28, 31a (**OT–1**) • Revelation 19:1, 5–9a (**NT–14**) • Matthew 5:1–12a (**G–1**)

The New Testament Readings

*In this section, you will find fourteen options from the
New Testament with commentaries to help you read
and reflect on them. If there is a Second Reading at your
wedding, you will choose from one of these readings. The
readings are numbered as **NT–1**, **NT–2**, and so on. (Note that
the reading from Revelation **(NT–14)** should be used as your
First Reading during Easter Time.) One reading for your
wedding liturgy must be about Marriage. These readings
have been marked with an asterisk.*

*The New Testament includes twenty-one letters written to
early Christian communities. Thirteen of these letters are
attributed to St. Paul. Three more are attributed to St. John.
Still others are attributed to Sts. Peter, James, and Jude.
Many of the letters were written in response to a particular
challenge that had arisen in that community. Some of the
letters raise questions for contemporary readers, especially
when they speak about issues like slavery or the place
of women in society. Knowing the context is important in
understanding where the writer is coming from and what
the letters have to say to us today. Most of all, though, the
letters are filled with practical and spiritual wisdom.*

*As you select one Second Reading for your wedding, read
each passage and its commentary carefully. What does the
reading have to say about love—our love for each other and
God's love for us? Which reading most expresses the kind
of love you want to have for each other? You will notice
some readings have a long form and a short form to choose.
The short form is in brackets. Record your Second Reading
selection on the form on **page 92** and give it to your priest
or deacon.*

NT–1 *What will separate us from the love of Christ?*

A reading from the Letter of Saint Paul to the Romans

8:31b–35, 37–39

Brothers and sisters:
If God is for us, who can be against us?
He did not spare his own Son
    but handed him over for us all,
      will he not also give us everything else along with him?
Who will bring a charge against God's chosen ones?
It is God who acquits us.
Who will condemn?
It is Christ Jesus who died, rather, was raised,
    who also is a the right hand of God,
      who indeed intercedes for us.
What will separate us from the love of Christ?
Will anguish, or distress, or persecution, or famine,
    or nakedness, or peril, or the sword?

No, in all these things, we conquer overwhelmingly
    through him who loved us.
For I am convinced that neither death, nor life,
    nor angels, nor principalities,
    nor present things, nor future things,
    nor powers, nor height, nor depth,
    nor any other creature will be able to separate us
    from the love of God in Christ Jesus our Lord.

The word of the Lord.

You might select this reading because . . .
You trust in God that, no matter what happens, you and your spouse will stay together. • In your relationship, you have faced adversity and depended on God to help you through it as a couple. • Your faith is such that you know that nothing will keep you from the love of Christ, and that love will strengthen your relationship.

If you select this reading, you might also consider . . .
Jeremiah 31:31–32a, 33–34a (**OT–9**) • Psalm 33:12 and 18, 20–21, 22 (**RP–1***)* •
John 15:12–16 (**G–9**)

Background of the Reading

Couples who have stayed the course and remained married for years often speak of the ups and downs they have endured together. Times of transitions, financial challenges, raising children, and unexpected illness, all can shake a Marriage. Yet this reading from Paul to the Romans tells us that God's love in Christ is ours. Nothing that comes our way in life can defeat us when we live out of the belief that redemption in Christ Jesus is ours.

Paul's letter to the Romans is the longest and most theological of all his letters. In profound, but sometimes complicated, theological language, Paul teaches that Christ's redemptive work frees Christians from sin and death. Christ justifies and saves us. Christ redeems us. The grace of redemption he freely gives to all who believe.

If you as a couple choose this reading, see yourself respond to the opening rhetorical questions. If God is for us, no one can be against us; yes, God will give us everything else along with Christ Jesus, God's Son; no one will successfully charge or condemn God's chosen ones; nothing will separate us from the love of Christ; not even anguish or distress that will come our way will mean losing the love of God in Christ.

As a married couple, you will be able to conquer struggles that come your way. Christ will always intercede for you; Christ will always support you; Christ will always love you. What this reading does not say is that life in Christ will be easy. What this poetic, rhythmic passage does say is that God's love in Christ triumphs.

The final section lists everything that could possibly separate you from Christ's love. The reality that death, life, angels, principalities, present things, future things, powers, height, depth, creatures cannot and will not destroy the bond of Christ's love with you communicates just how strong his love truly is. Christ's love is so expansive and powerful that absolutely nothing can conquer it. All that is evil in the world will attempt to pull you as a couple from God and each other. Christ's love, though, will not allow this to happen. Your responsibility as a couple is to hold fast to Paul's advice to the Romans: cling to faith. Center your life in the deep, wide, everlasting, and beautiful love of Christ. In this love, God calls you to live as a married couple.

NT-2 *Offer your bodies as a living sacrifice, holy and pleasing to God.*

A reading from the Letter of Saint Paul to the Romans

Long form: 12:1–2, 9–18
[Short form: 12:1–2, 9–13]

[I urge you, brothers and sisters,
　　by the mercies of God,
　to offer your bodies as
　　a living sacrifice,
　holy and pleasing to God, your
　　spiritual worship.
Do not conform yourself to this age
　but be transformed by the re-
　　newal of your mind,
　that you may discern what is the
　　will of God,
　what is good and pleasing
　　and perfect.

Let love be sincere;
　hate what is evil,
　hold on to what is good;
　love one another with
　　mutual affection;
　anticipate one another in
　　showing honor.
Do not grow slack in zeal,
　be fervent in spirit,
　serve the Lord.

Rejoice in hope,
　endure in affliction,
　persevere in prayer.
Contribute to the needs
　of the holy ones,
　exercise hospitality.]
Bless those who persecute you,
　bless and do not curse them.
Rejoice with those who rejoice,
　Weep with those who weep.
Have the same regard for
　one another;
　do not be haughty but associate
　　with the lowly;
　do not be wise in your
　　own estimation.
Do not repay anyone evil for evil;
　be concerned for what is noble
　　in the sight of all.
If possible, on your own part,
　live at peace with all.

The word of the Lord.

You might select this reading because . . .
Your love is so grounded in Christ that you are steadfast in hope and prayer, even when your journey is rough. • You are not content to live as many do in this age, clinging to the material. • As a couple, you strive for mutual affection and still reach out to others in hospitality and compassion.

If you select this reading, you might also consider . . .
Proverbs 31:10–13, 19–20, 30–31 **(OT–6)** • Psalm 112:1bc–2, 3–4, 5–7a, 7bc–8, 9 **(RP–4)** • Matthew 5:1–12a **(G–1)**

Background of the Reading

What does it mean for Christians to present their "bodies as a living sacrifice"? Prior to the time of Christ, the law of Moses included the primary guidelines for how to live as God's people. Paul teaches that with Christ's gift of salvation, now people themselves are to present themselves as living sacrifices. No longer do Christians have to follow the letter of the law in offering ritual sacrifices. Cultic observances do not govern the Christian life; animal sacrifices are obsolete. God's gift of justification and love in Christ Jesus is the basis for how Christians live.

For Paul, "body" referred not just to one's physical being, but to one's entire person. To be a "living sacrifice," then, means to make your entire person, mind, body, and soul available to another. We are living sacrifices for one another when we work to maintain the unity of our relationships and the unity of the Christian community. Hope, prayer, hospitality, rejoicing, weeping, equality, mutuality, having the same regard for one another, our outreach to the lowly, and the forgiving manner in which we respond when someone wrongs us, are all characteristics of relationships modeled on Christ's redemptive sacrifice.

The emphasis of this reading on sincere love is an appropriate proclamation in the wedding liturgy because it focuses you, the couple, on how to respond in love to your spouse and also to have a united response to various situations that might arise in your life together. How you discern together what it means to engage in a common pursuit of the good will define how you offer yourselves as a living sacrifice. Paul always sees Christ Jesus as the model for our living sacrifice. This reading asks you as a couple to follow his example, even though you most likely will not have to give your life as he did.

In this passage, Paul speaks not about a shallow or outward change regarding how Christians relate to others. Nor does he speak about Christians adapting the passing and imperfect model for relationships that belongs to this world and this age. Paul instead speaks about a profound, internal conversion to Christ Jesus that brands Christian love as a living sacrifice modeled on Christ's own sacrifice. This is the love that compels you as a couple to live at peace with all, and to approach the choices you will need to make in your Marriage with the mind of Christ.

NT-3 *Welcome one another as Christ welcomed you.*

A reading from the Letter of Saint Paul to the Romans

15:1b–3a, 5–7, 13

Brothers and sisters:
We ought to put up with the failings of the weak and not to please ourselves;
    let each of us please our neighbor for the good,
    for building up.
For Christ did not please himself.
May the God of endurance and encouragement
    grant you to think in harmony with one another,
    in keeping with Christ Jesus,
    that with one accord you may with one voice
    glorify the God and Father of our Lord Jesus Christ.

Welcome one another, then, as Christ welcomed you,
    for the glory of God.
May the God of hope fill you with all joy and peace in believing,
    so that you may abound in hope by the power of the Holy Spirit.

The Word of the Lord.

You might select this reading because . . .
Hospitality is at your core so much so that you welcome, and do not take for granted, anyone. • You seek for each person to have a say in order that a consensus can be reached in a decision. • As a couple, you see Christ at the center of your Marriage helping you build each other up.

If you select this reading, you might also consider . . .
Song of Songs 2:8–10, 14, 16a; 8:6–7a (**OT–7**) • Psalm 103:1–2, 8 and 13, 17–18a (**RP–3**) • Matthew 22:35–40 (**G–5**)

Background of the Reading

This passage comes from the latter part of Paul's letter to the Romans. The conflict between the weak and the strong often evident in Paul's letters presents itself at the beginning of the reading. Paul's response to the conflict emphasizes unity through hospitality.

Christian love for one another finds its inspiration in Christ's love for us. Christ himself was a person for others; he did not strive to please himself above everyone else. Christ's sacrifice on the Cross is the highest example of this.

Paul teaches that when we follow the example of Christ in our relationships, we build up the common good. Pleasing others creates harmony rather than discord in our communities. Harmony, it is important to note, does not mean that we all think and act exactly like one another in order to live peaceably. Harmony among Christians and their neighbors is akin to living in openness to one another, creating the space for thoughtfully considering others' views and allowing others to live as God's people.

For Paul, Christians think in harmony with others by thinking with the mind of Christ. This means always considering how we model our lives on the life of Christ. It means asking how we, in our relationships, can welcome each other, as Christ constantly welcomes us into his love.

Paul knows that the job of welcoming others is not easy. He ends this passage with a prayer. His prayer recognizes how God's presence extends endurance, encouragement, and hope as we continually seek unity in our relationships and communities. His prayer is a blessing for all people as they seek ways to let Christ's love motivate them in their relationships.

In your relationship with each other, Paul would advise you to seek to please others as Christ did, but not to become people pleasers. Living in unity and harmony with each other does not mean either spouse will get his or her way all the time. It means working together as a couple to discover how you can make God's love present in ways that honor the other person, while at the same time recognizing both of you are children of God. The ultimate sign of glorifying God in your Marriage relationship is welcoming your spouse—even when you have had the longest possible day you can imagine! God will gift you with hope, joy, and peace as you live out this mission of hospitality in your relationship—all for the good.

NT-4 *Your body is a temple of the Spirit.*

A reading from the first Letter of Saint Paul to the Corinthians
6:13c–15a, 17–20

Brothers and sisters:
The body is not for immorality, but for the Lord,
>   and the Lord is for the body;
>   God raised the Lord and will also raise us by his power.

Do you not know that your bodies are members of Christ?
Whoever is joined to the Lord becomes one spirit with him.

Avoid immorality.
Every other sin a person commits is outside the body,
>   but the immoral person sins against his own body.
Do you not know that your body
>   is a temple of the Holy Spirit within you,
>   whom you have from God, and that you are not your own?
For you have been purchased at a price.
Therefore glorify God in your body.

The word of the Lord.

You might select this reading because . . .
You understand that your intimate union in Marriage is grounded in Christ's love
for you. • Your treatment of your body is rooted in the fact that it is a temple of
the Holy Spirit. • Through your diet and activities, you have treated your body as
a gift from God.

If you select this reading, you might also consider . . .
Tobit 8:4b–8 (**OT–5**) • Psalm 128:1–2, 3, 4–5ac and 6a (**RP–5**) • Mark 10:6–9 (**G–6**)

Background of the Reading

At the time Paul wrote his letter, the Christian community at Corinth was dealing with many conflicts. Corinth was a bustling cosmopolitan seaport of people from various ethnic and religious backgrounds, different socio-economic classes, who held divergent views on what was immoral. In the verses that precede the beginning of this reading, Paul is clear about what are immoral actions for Christians: fornication, idolatry, adultery, and drunkenness because of which people will not inherit the Kingdom of God.

Paul teaches that through Baptism, Christians have been sanctified and washed clean. For Paul, Christians were to act differently than those people in Corinth who chose immorality and licentiousness over morality and regard for self and others. Morality for Christians involves the body. And, the body is not only the physical body and its desires. For Paul, the body involves one's entire life—how one thinks and acts, how one feels and relates to one's self, others, and to God.

The Christian body is the temple of the Holy Spirit. The Holy Spirit infuses every cell of the human body and animates the person to do good, to choose morality over immorality. God owns the body; the Holy Spirit lives within the body; and through the saving Death and Resurrection of Jesus' own body, he sanctifies the body so that it no longer belongs wholly to the human person, it belongs to God. The relationship of the human body to God, for Paul, is trinitarian: the body belongs to God through Jesus Christ in the Holy Spirit.

As an engaged couple preparing for your wedding liturgy, what is important to reflect on in this reading is that both of your bodies belong to Christ; you do not belong to each other. You are both children of God. Sexuality is the very intimate way you express your relationship with each other and with God. God calls you as a couple to avoid immorality and embrace morality. In doing so, you as a couple act on Paul's concluding, positive instruction to glorify God in your body.

God calls you to respect the holiness of each other's body—each other's entire person—through how you act and present yourselves in your relationship to each other and to the world. Each of your bodies is a temple of the Holy Spirit. How you will communicate with each other through your bodies to glorify God in your married life together is what these words of Paul ask you to consider prayerfully.

NT-5 *If I do not have love, I gain nothing.*

A reading from the first Letter of Saint Paul to the Corinthians

12:31 — 13:8a

Brothers and sisters:
Strive eagerly for the greatest spiritual gifts.

But I shall show you a still more excellent way.

If I speak in human and angelic tongues
    but do not have love,
       I am a resounding gong or a clashing cymbal.
And if I have the gift of prophecy
    and comprehend all mysteries and all knowledge;
       if I have all faith so as to move mountains,
       but do not have love, I am nothing.
If I give away everything I own,
    and If I had my body over so that I may boast
       but do not have love, I gain nothing.

Love is patient, love is kind.
It is not jealous, it is not pompous,
    it is not inflated, it is not rude,
    it does not seek its own interests,
    it is not quick-tempered, it does not brood over
       injury, it does not rejoice over wrongdoing
    but rejoices with the truth.
It bears all things, believes all things,
    hopes all things, endures all things.
Love never fails.

The word of the Lord.

You might select this reading because . . .
You consider love to be a gift from God to be shared with others. • As a couple,
you have looked to your love for each other to get you through hardships. •
You cherish your relationship enough to seek to be patient and kind, knowing
that small sacrifices promote your love.

If you select this reading, you might also consider . . .
Song of Songs 2:8–10, 14, 16a; 8:6–7a (**OT–7**) • Psalm 148:1–2, 3–4, 9–10, 11–13a,
13c–14a (**RP–7**) • Matthew 22:35–40 (**G–5**)

Background of the Reading

With love, you are beautiful music. With love, you are everything. With love, you acquire everything. These are the corollaries to the three negative statements at the end of each "if" statement in the first half of this passage. Love indeed is everything, according to Paul's teaching to the Corinthians. Herein lies the reason this reading is beloved and so frequently selected by couples for their Marriage liturgy.

The love Paul speaks about in this reading is agape, not eros or sexual love, not philos or friendship, but true self-giving love that authenticates another's personhood as divine gift. This is the love in Christ Jesus that endures forever and ever. This is love that does not let another person down. This is the love that makes possible the resolution of conflicts in relationships. This love is nothing less than the greatest gift of the Spirit.

For Paul, agape is the opposite of the discordant and contentious spirit evident among the Corinthians. Unfettered pride and selfishness caused disunity between the strong and weak in the Corinthian community. Arrogance related to the ordering of spiritual gifts caused dissent. In contrast, Paul's poetic and flowing description of love describes the significance of love—that which love is capable of doing.

Paul begins by listing the spiritual gifts that are causing controversy among the Corinthians. He orders them in reverse order from what the Corinthians would, beginning with the gift of tongues in the lowest position. He proceeds to name other spiritual gifts such as prophecy and self-sacrifice. Paul, himself, wanted the Corinthians to value all spiritual gifts equally, while at the same time recognizing the diversity of the gifts the Spirit gives. All gifts are for the building up of the Christian community in Christ Jesus.

Paul's concluding statement in the reading, "Love never fails," actually serves as an introduction to the next section in his letter. In this section, he tells the Corinthians that many other gifts do not last. The triad of faith, hope, and love will remain, but it is love that is the greatest. You will probably know love is the greatest gift even before you grow old together. Often, people remark how the first years of Marriage can be the most challenging. Your love is a gift from God to you. God intends you to share your love with others whom your life together touches.

NT-6 *One Body and one Spirit.*

A reading from the first Letter of Saint Paul to the Ephesians

4:1–6

Brothers and sisters:
I, then, a prisoner for the Lord,
    urge you to live in a manner worthy of the call you have received,
    with all humility and gentleness, with patience,
    bearing with one another through love,
    striving to preserve the unity of the spirit through the bond of peace:
    one Body and one Spirit,
    as you were also called to the one hope of your call;
    one Lord, one faith, one baptism;
    one God and Father of all,
    who is over all and through all and in all.

The word of the Lord.

You might select this reading because . . .
You have a devotion to St. Francis, who lived a life of humility, gentleness,
and peace. • As a couple, you have been involved in organizations that promote
peace. • The Beatitude that begins, "Blessed are the peacemakers" is close to
your hearts.

If you select this reading, you might also consider . . .
Jeremiah 31:31–32a, 33–34a **(OT–9)** • Psalm 34:2–3, 4–5, 6–7, 8–9 **(RP–2)** •
John 17:20–26 **(G–10)**

Background of the Reading

By choosing to celebrate the Sacrament of Matrimony, you as a couple acknowledge God's call in your lives. God called you through Baptism to live as God's adopted son and daughter. God now calls you to live out your baptismal call through your relationship of married love with each other. The living out of your baptismal call through the Sacrament of Matrimony will be a lot of work. Unity, the theme of this reading, will be an important theme of sacramental Marriage as well.

Paul writes to the Universal Church in his letter to the Ephesians, not to a specific local community. His main concern is how people will live the Christian life in the world. The verses of this reading, which come from the beginning of chapter 4, emphasize the unity of all in the one Body of Christ, the Church. Notice in the reading that this unity is sevenfold; Paul uses the word "one" seven times in reference to unity.

The three "ones" acknowledging the singleness and uniqueness of the Lord, our faith, and Baptism also remind us of the Triune nature of our faith. These three "ones" are important in many of the Church's creeds throughout history. All seven of the unity phrases build to a conclusion that affirms the oneness of God who is Father and whose being permeates creation and humankind.

When you reflect on the reading, think about how Paul instructs the people of the Church to practice their faith. Let humility and gentleness, patience and mutual support of one another, and love for each other guide your relationship with each other. Choose to cultivate the unity of your relationship based on mutual faith through peace. Marriage isn't always easy, and some days it can be difficult to communicate effectively. This reading reminds us about the one faith to which God calls us, and emphasizes that you have the one Church of faith, the Body of Christ, to support you as you live out your baptismal call through the Sacrament of Matrimony.

Living in unity with your spouse and the Church does not mean that everyone does things the same way, as it did for Paul when he instructed the Ephesians. Paul recognized that unity in the Church is maintained and preserved best when people use the variety of gifts God generously gives them. Allow your unique gifts to shine forth as you live out your relationship with each other. In so doing, you will build up the Body of Christ and all God's world around you.

NT-7 *This is a great mystery, but I speak in reference to Christ and the Church.*

A reading from the Letter of Saint Paul to the Ephesians

Long form: 5:2a, 21–33*
[Short form: 5:2a, 25–32*]

[Brothers and sisters:
Live in love, as Christ loved us
    and handed himself over for us.]

Be subordinate to one another
        out of reverence for Christ.
Wives should be subordinate
        to their husbands as to
        the Lord.
For the husband is the head
        of his wife
    just as Christ is head
        of the Church,
    he himself the savior of the body.
As the Church is subordinate
        to Christ,
    so wives should be subordinate
    to their husbands in
        everything.
[Husbands, love your wives,
    even as Christ loved the Church
    and handed himself over
        for her to sanctify her,
    cleansing her by the bath
        of water with the word,
    that he might present to himself
        the Church in splendor,

without spot or wrinkle or any
        such thing,
    that she might be holy
        and without blemish.
So also husbands should love
        their wives as their
        own bodies.
He who loves his wife loves himself.
For no one hates his own flesh
        but rather nourishes and
        cherishes it,
    even as Christ does the Church,
    because we are members
        of his Body.

*For this reason a man shall
        leave his father and
        his mother
    and be joined to his wife,
    and the two shall become
        one flesh.*

This is a great mystery,
        but I speak in reference to Christ
        and the Church.]
In any case, each one of you should
        love his wife as himself,
    and the wife should respect
        her husband.

The word of the Lord.

You might select this reading because . . .
You look to the way that Christ loves the Church as how you will love each other in Marriage. • As a couple, you seek unity, as Christ does with his Church. • You would like to meditate on the implications of the Church as the bride of Christ.

If you select this reading, you might also consider . . .
Proverbs 31:10–13, 19–20, 30–31 (OT–6) • Psalm 128:1–2, 3, 4–5ac and 6a (RP–5) • Matthew 19:3–6 (G–4)

Background of the Reading

The focus of Ephesians is the Church. The Church in Ephesians is not the local church, as it is in many of Paul's letters, but rather the Universal Church. Christ is the head of the Church, his Body, whose mission is to make God's saving love in Jesus Christ known to all. The reading continues with specific directives on how husbands and wives are to order their relationship of love with one another. These directives are part of an ancient household code. Household codes were instructions for daily living that were prevalent in Greco-Roman philosophy. New Testament authors adapted them for their purposes. In this case, the household code helps the author of Ephesians to articulate the relationship between husband and wife in terms of the relationship between Christ and the Church.

Household codes always began by listing the duties of the "inferior" person first, the "superior" last. Today, we are not to take this stratification literally. In the latter part of the first century, household codes also functioned to show how Christianity did not detract from the hierarchical ordering of Greco-Roman society. The emphasis of Christianity on equality within the Body of Christ, the Church—among men and women, rich and poor, slave and free— often left Christians open to the charge that they were creating discord in society. One way to counter this accusation was for New Testament authors to adopt the household codes and then describe them in light of the proclamation of Jesus Christ and his love for the Church and world.

The husband's instructions on how to love his wife include a scriptural reference to Genesis showing how God calls a man and woman to the married life. The instructions also embrace a strong call to mutual love between husband and wife as exemplified in the love between Christ and the Church. The husband models his love for his wife on Christ's love for the Church, his own Body.

The "great mystery" at the conclusion of this reading is the mystery of Christ's love for the Church and how it serves as the model for spousal love. The unity of man and woman mirrors the unity and love of Christ and the Church. As a couple, your daily living out of your love for each other will make known the great mystery of Christ's love for the Church. Your mutual love for each and your sharing of that love through the Church makes Christ's love known to the world today.

A reading from the Letter of Saint Paul to the Philippians *4:4–9*

Brothers and sisters:
Rejoice in the Lord always.
I shall say it again: rejoice!
Your kindness should be known to all.
The Lord is near.
Have no anxiety at all, but in everything,
 by prayer and petition, with thanksgiving,
 make your requests known to God.
Then the peace of God that surpasses all understanding
 will guard your hearts and minds in Christ Jesus.

Finally, brothers and sisters,
 whatever is true, whatever is honorable,
 whatever is just, whatever is pure,
 whatever is lovely, whatever is gracious,
 if there is any excellence
 and if there is anything worthy of praise,
 think about these things.
Keep on doing what you have learned and received
 and heard and seen in me.
Then the God of peace will be with you.

The word of the Lord.

You might select this reading because . . .
You seek to rejoice in all circumstances. • As a couple, you seek to perform small
kindnesses to each other and those you meet, knowing that shows your love. •
Your faith is such that you are able to see past difficult times and set aside anxiety.

If you select this reading, you might also consider . . .
Jeremiah 31:31–32a, 33–34a (**OT–9**) • Psalm 128:1–2, 3, 4–5ac and 6a (**RP–5**) •
Matthew 5:13–16 (**G–2**)

Background of the Reading

You might recognize this reading from Advent. In Year C, on the Third Sunday of the season of preparation for Christmas, we hear the same call to "Rejoice." The call comes from Paul in the final chapter of his letter to the Philippians, a people with whom he had a close and endearing relationship. Paul wrote to the Philippians encouraging them to persevere in the faith. The Christian community at Philippi faced opposition because of their proclamation of the Gospel. At times, the Philippians faced the threat of persecution, even death.

Paul wrote to the Philippians from prison as he awaited his own trial. The focus of the letter, however, is not his own situation. In this letter, as in his other letters, Paul reminds Christians of the importance of the Gospel. Salvation that belongs to Christians through Jesus Christ is the reason to rejoice. The Lord saves through the Gospel of death and resurrection. This compels us to rejoice *always*, even when situations might lead us to do the opposite.

The instructions to the Philippians found in this reading are appropriate instructions for a couple to hear at their wedding liturgy as well. As a married couple you are to live together in such a way that everyone knows your kindness. You will have anxiety, but God will ease it as you make your requests known to God and offer thanksgiving in return for all God will do for you.

When you live with gratefulness and generosity, you will experience the peace of God that Paul mentions. It is a peace that extends beyond the limits of our human understanding. The peace is a divine peace that comes from God in Christ Jesus. This is why in the concluding line of the reading Paul turns the phrase "peace of God" around to read the "God of peace."

The God of peace will accompany you throughout the journey of your married life. You as a couple can probably already name occasions in which you have experienced the God of peace. Let these experiences be the basis for the challenging times in your life, when peace seems absent. Strive to follow Paul's other instructions to the Philippians that he derives from ancient Greco-Roman philosophy: consider what is true, honorable, just, pure, lovely, and gracious. A life lived by these virtues will lead you deeper into unity with the God of peace.

NT-9 *And over all these put on love, that is,*
the bond of perfection.

A reading from the Letter of Saint Paul to the Colossians

3:12–17

Brothers and sisters:
Put on, as God's chosen ones, holy and beloved,
heartfelt compassion, kindness, humility, gentleness, and patience,
bearing with one another and forgiving one another,
if one has a grievance against another;
as the Lord has forgiven you, so must you also do.
And over all these put on love,
that is, the bond of perfection.
And let the peace of Christ control your hearts,
the peace into which you were also called in one Body.
And be thankful.
Let the word of Christ dwell in you richly,
as in all wisdom you teach and admonish one another,
singing psalms, hymns, and spiritual songs
with gratitude in your hearts to God.
And whatever you do, in word or in deed,
do everything in the name of the Lord Jesus,
giving thanks to God the Father through him.

The word of the Lord.

You might select this reading because . . .
You have gratitude for your relationship and all God has given you. • You strive to
live gently and patiently and understand the power of forgiveness. • A great wrong
has happened to you at some point and you have known the peace that comes
with forgiveness and reconciliation.

If you select this reading, you might also consider . . .
Tobit 8:4b–8 (**OT–5**) • Psalm 145:8–9, 10 and 15, 17–18 (**RP–6**) •
Matthew 5:1–12a (**G–1**)

Background of the Reading

In response to their false teachings, the letter to the Colossians defines what constitutes faithful and authentic Christian life. Earlier in Colossians 3, Paul reminds them and us that authentic self-discipline involves overcoming our own personal sin. Our reading begins with the second dimension of the true Christian life, putting on love.

While Colossians 3:5–8 includes two lists of five vices each, this reading includes a list of virtues. These are the virtues of an authentic Christian life lived in the name of Christ Jesus. Read in the context of the wedding liturgy, they are the virtues God calls a husband and wife to "put on" in their relationship. They are the virtues of married life and family life, which is why this reading is also proclaimed on the Feast of the Holy Family of Jesus, Mary, and Joseph during Christmas Time.

The phrase "put on" could be a reference to the new life Christians "put on" in Baptism. In this sacrament, God's grace washes away our old life. As God's chosen and beloved, we embrace the call to live according to the virtues of compassion, kindness, humility, gentleness, and patience. We acknowledge that in Baptism we become a new creation.

The Lord who has forgiven us, now calls us to forgive others when we have grievances. Just as God calls us to the Lord's example of forgiveness, so too, God's call extends to imitating his love. Nothing is more perfect than love that is ever expanding and ever deepening, moving closer and closer to the Lord's own love.

The reading also encourages Christians to allow the peace of Christ into their hearts to rule and guide their decisions. As a couple, God calls you into this peace just as God calls the Church, the Body of Christ into peace. God calls you to allow his Word to reside in you, to worship together, and to seek wisdom together. God calls you to live in gratitude.

Neither the Christian life nor the married life is a solo venture; no one person has to go it alone figuring out how to live a faithful, authentic, and virtuous life. This couples do together with the support of the Christian community, the Church. And this, as the final line of the reading tells us, Christians do in the name of the Lord Jesus, grateful for all that God has already done in him for us and all that God will do in the future.

NT–10 *Let marriage be held in honor by all.*

A reading from the Letter to the Hebrews   *13:1–4a, 5–6b*

Brothers and sisters:
Let mutual love continue.
Do not neglect hospitality,
    for through it some have unknowingly entertained angels.
Be mindful of prisoners as if sharing their imprisonment,
    and of the ill-treated as of yourselves,
    for you also are in the body.
Let marriage be honored among all
    and the marriage bed be kept undefiled.
Let your life be free from love of money
    but be content with what you have,
    for he has said, *I will never forsake you or abandon you.*
Thus we may say with confidence:

      The Lord is my helper,
      and I will not be afraid.

The word of the Lord.

You might select this reading because . . .
As a couple, you seek to live simply because, by living with less, others can have more. • Through your work in the community, you consider the needs of others. • You are a minister of hospitality in the parish or your job requires you to look into the needs and comforts of others.

If you select this reading, you might also consider . . .
Tobit 7:6–14 **(OT–4)** • Psalm 112:1bc–2, 3–4, 5–7a, 7bc–8, 9 **(RP–4)** • John 2:1–11 **(G–7)**

Background of the Reading

Paul wrote the letter to the Hebrews as a source of encouragement for Jewish Christians who were tired with the requirements of the Christian life. The ultimate encouragement for Christians is found in Jesus' own sacrifice. His sacrifice teaches us that in the end, the struggle does not remain. The grace of eternal joy and eternal victory are not only his, but ours. Hebrews focuses us not only on the example par excellence of Jesus' own life, but on the lives of those who have gone before us in the faith from the Old Testament (11:1–40). We are never alone on the pilgrimage of faith. Married couples will never be alone as they strive to live according to the specific moral instructions provided in this reading.

In this reading, Paul communicates moral commandments that go hand in hand with living as Christians in the world. The call to mutual love, hospitality, empathy for prisoners and the ill-treated is idealistic and beautiful, yet immensely difficult to embrace. Paul instructs Christians to honor Marriage and to recognize the goodness inherent in the relationship between husband and wife. He reminds the married couple to honor the intimacy of their relationships as expressed in sexuality. He instructs Christians to resist the love of money and, instead, choose contentment—satisfaction with the material possessions that they have.

As he communicates these moral instructions, Paul not only assures the Hebrews, but we who follow in their footsteps of faith, that God is always with us, helping us to live out our faith in the midst of daily life. Paul offers this assurance by quoting two Old Testament sources with which his readers would have familiarity: Joshua 1:5 and Psalm 118:6. The first reminds them God never leaves God's people behind. The second tells us simply that God is there to help and because of this, we do not have to be afraid.

In the context of the wedding liturgy, these two Old Testament citations offer you as a newly married couple the confidence to go forward on your journey, embracing the demands of the Christian life. They also remind you as a couple to call on the Lord through prayer, using the texts of Scripture to strengthen your faith, just as believers have done for centuries. Through prayer, you will know God's help as you live what it means to follow the moral commandments of this reading in the twenty-first century.

NT–11 *Be of one mind, sympathetic, loving toward one another.*

A reading from the first Letter of Saint Peter   *3:1–9**

Beloved:
You wives should be subordinate to your husbands so that,
    even if some disobey the word,
    they may be won over without a word by their wives' conduct
    when they observe your reverent and chaste behavior.
Your adornment should not be an external one:
    braiding the hair, wearing gold jewelry, or dressing in fine clothes,
    but rather the hidden character of the heart,
    expressed in the imperishable beauty
    of a gentle and calm disposition,
    which is precious in the sight of God.
For this is also how the holy women who hoped in God
    once used to adorn themselves
    and were subordinate to their husbands;
    thus Sarah obeyed Abraman, calling him "lord."
You are her children when you do what is good
    and fear no intimidation.

Likewise, you husbands should live with your wives in understanding,
    showing honor to the weaker female sex,
    since we are joint heirs of the gifts of life,
    so that your prayers may not be hindered.

Finally, all of you, be of one mind, sympathetic,
    loving toward one another, compassionate, humble.
Do not return evil for evil, or insult for insult;
    but, on the contrary, a blessing, because to this you were called,
    that you might inherit a blessing.

The word of the Lord.

You might select this reading because . . .
You live as though your interior life is more important than the external. •
As a couple, you know the value of honoring each other. • You seek to live
as a peacemaker, and overlook insult and seek good for all.

If you select this reading, you might also consider . . .
Proverbs 31:10–13, 19–20, 30–31 (OT–6) • Psalm 103:1–2, 8 and 13, 17–18a
(RP–3) • Matthew 22:35–40 (G–5)

Background of the Reading

There are three distinct sections in this reading. The first section provides instructions for the wife, the second for the husband, and the third for all believers. First Peter is a pastoral letter of encouragement to Christians in five provinces of Asia Minor in the middle to late first century. Many of the Christians in these communities are new Gentile (non-Jewish) converts. These fledgling Christians now face persecution because of their faith and the moral conduct required by it.

We understand the moral instructions in this reading option for the wedding liturgy in light of the first-century world. The instructions for the husband and wife are commonly seen in household codes in the ancient world. We can find similar instructions in other books of the New Testament, such as Colossians and Ephesians. The first century world and its social fabric was patriarchal. Women were considered the weaker sex. While the reading reiterates this, the focus of the first section is on the interior conversion of the woman. What she wears or how she looks is not important. The character of her heart is. In this, her life of faith is similar to the great ancestors of faith like Sarah. The wife's interior conversion is what influences her husband.

The second section of the reading instructs husbands to live in understanding with their wives, honoring them. The reading does not advise the husbands further. For Christians, both husbands and wives are heirs to the promise of eternal life in Christ. The Christian reality that husbands and wives are joint heirs of the gifts of life was new to the ancient world. The love of Christ now formed the social code from patriarchal society that ordered Marriage.

The third section of the reading reminds us that God calls all Christians to be of one mind. This one mind is not a generic mind, but is the mind of Christ. In him and through him, we see and experience the sympathy, love, compassion, and humility God asks us to live. God calls us to be a blessing so that God's blessing in Christ will forever be ours. As husband and wife to be, this call to be a blessing is yours. Be a blessing to each other, to your friends and family, to co–workers and strangers, to the world. Each day of your married life, let this reading remind you to unify your minds with Christ's mind. Together, you will inherit the gift of life.

NT–12 *Love in deed and in truth.*

A reading from the first Letter of Saint John   *3:18–24*

Children, let us love not in word or speech
    but in deed and truth.

Now this is how we shall know that we belong to the truth
    and reassure our hearts before him
    in whatever our hearts condemn,
    for God is greater than our hearts and knows everything.
Beloved, if our hearts do not condemn us,
    we have confidence in God
    and receive from him whatever we ask,
    because we keep his commandments and do what pleases him.
And his commandment is this:
    we should believe in the name of his Son, Jesus Christ,
    and love one another just as he commanded us.
Those who keep his commandments remain in him, and he in them,
    and the way we know that he remains in us
    is from the Spirit that he gave us.

The word of the Lord.

You might select this reading because . . .
You seek not to judge yourself or others harshly, knowing that God does not judge us harshly if we seek to do his will. • In your daily life, your focus is to live the way Christ commanded us. • As a couple, you plan to center your home life on prayer and keep Christ as the center.

If you select this reading, you might also consider . . .
Sirach 26:1–4, 13–16 (**OT–8**) • Psalm 128:1–2, 3, 4–5ac and 6a (**RP–5**) • John 17:20–26 (**G–10**)

Background of the Reading

How often have we said to someone (or someone said to us), "Your actions do not match your words"? Consistency matters. The author of the First Letter of John communicates this truth to his readers. Written around the turn of the first century, this letter refutes false teachings about Jesus Christ. Some people believed that Jesus was not the Christ and rejected his true divinity; others denied the fullness of his humanity. These false beliefs led the author of 1 John to present the importance of the unity of belief and action.

The words we speak must match our actions. If we profess belief in Jesus Christ and the saving love that is ours through his Death and Resurrection, we must live a life of love modeled on Christ's love for us. Our love for one another in Christ reveals the truth of salvation that is ours through God's Son. Faith and love exist together. Believing the truth about Jesus Christ and his love for us goes hand in hand with loving others.

This reading also teaches us that our hearts are not even capable of condemning ourselves or others if we believe rightly in God and keep God's commandments. The commandment is twofold: believe rightly in Jesus Christ *and* love according to Jesus' own command. God's eternal and infinite capacity to forgive even when we fall short of professing and living his commandment is what keeps us from judging others and ourselves too harshly. Have confidence in God, the author of 1 John tells us, because we are God's children. God knows how we strive to love in deed and in truth, though at times we fall short of the ideal.

Still, we can be certain of God's love and confident that we remain united with Jesus Christ through the gift of the Spirit. There will be times in the Marriage relationship that you fall short of your spouse's expectations. You will disappoint each other. This is when forgiveness is necessary. Neither partner will ever reach perfection in loving the other or loving God. There will be times when each spouse is frustrated with the other because their actions do not match their words. Your ongoing love for one another and confidence in God's ongoing love in Jesus Christ will not take away your frustration, but it will announce hope instead of condemnation. The assurance of God's love will allow you to continue to love each other as husband and wife every day.

NT–13 *God is love.*

A reading from the first Letter of Saint John   *4:7–12*

Beloved, let us love one another,
>	because love is of God;
>	everyone who loves is begotten by God and knows God.

Whoever is without love does not know God, for God is love.

In this way the love of God was revealed to us:
>	God sent his only-begotten Son into the world
>	so that we might have life through him.

In this is love:
>	not that we have loved God, but that he loved us
>	and sent his Son as expiation for our sins.

Beloved, if God so loved us,
>	we also must love one another.

No one has ever seen God.

Yet, if we love one another, God remains in us,
>	and his love is brought to perfection in us.

The word of the Lord.

You might select this reading because . . .
Your faith assures you that God has loved us in our failings and that we are to love others even when their actions disappoint us. • You understand that God's love empowers you to love. • You believe God's love is brought to perfection in your relationship.

If you select this reading, you might also consider . . .
Song of Songs 2:8–10, 14, 16a; 8:6–7a **(OT–7)** • Psalm 112:1bc–2, 3–4, 5–7a, 7bc–8, 9 **(RP–4)** • John 15:12–16 **(G–9)**

Background of the Reading

Love. When we take this word at face value it appears so simple. God is love. God loves us through his Son. We love others. We love our spouse. We love our friends. We love our neighbors. If we do not love, we separate ourselves from our spouse and from our friends and neighbors. We do not know God. This passage from the first Letter of Saint John helps us understand how deep, profound, and lasting Christian love is because it comes from God.

We hear this passage proclaimed in Year A of the Lectionary cycle of readings on the Solemnity of the Most Sacred Heart of Jesus because this reading affirms the depth of Jesus' love for us. That God sent his Son as "expiation" for our sins means God loved us so much that the one sacrifice of his Son made amends for all sin. Jesus gave his life as forgiveness for our sins, even our sin of failing to love in a way that reflects God's love to another person and to the world. God's love is given freely through Jesus Christ. We are responsible to proclaim that love to the world through our love for one another.

Your love as husband and wife is a sign of God's presence in your lives. Your love witnesses to your friends and neighbors, to your coworkers, and to strangers of God's love for them. Your relationship with each other reveals God's presence. Your participation in the Church community makes the ongoing truth of God's love known to people of faith. It bolsters them to continue to live out God's love in their homes and places of work.

Let the conclusion of this reading inspire you to never stop loving each other, for God will always remain in you. Take from this reading the fact that God always loves. Despite the times when you might not love as you should or could, God's love for you remains. That is the truth of God's forgiveness expressed on the Cross through his Son. Let your love for each other embrace the forgiveness and constancy of God's love. Let God's love empower you to find particular ways that you as a couple can witness to divine love. Love, then, is not so simple, so plain, so easily described, for it is the magnificence of God's love being perfected in us.

NT–14 *Blessed are those who have been called to the wedding feast of the Lamb.*

A reading from the Book of Revelation   *19:1, 5–9a*

I, John, heard what sounded like the loud voice
    of a great multitude in heaven, saying:

> "Alleuia!
> Salvation, glory, and might belong to our God."

A voice coming from the throne said:

> "Praise our God, all you his servants,
>   and you who revere him, small and great."

Then I heard something like the sound of a great multitude
    or the sound of rushing water or mighty peals of thunder,
    as they said: "Alleluia!
    The Lord has established his reign, our God, the almighty.
    Let us rejoice and be glad and give him glory.
    For the wedding day of the Lamb has come,
        his bride has made herself ready.
    She was allowed to wear a bright, clean linen garment."
(The linen represents the righteous deeds of the holy ones.)

Then the angel said to me,
    "Write this:
    Blessed are those who have been called
    to the wedding feast of the Lamb."

The word of the Lord.

You might select this reading because . . .
You seek to make your love for each other symbolize the love God has for the Church. • As a couple, you have prepared through prayer for the Sacrament of Matrimony. • You understand that the wedding is not your day alone but a sacrament witnessed by all of heaven.

If you select this reading, you might also consider . . .
Tobit 7:6–14 (**OT–4**) • Psalm 34:2–3, 4–5, 6–7, 8–9 (**RP–2**) • John 2:1–11 (**G–7**)

Background of the Reading

The reference to the wedding feast of the Lamb is the clear connection to why this reading is an option for the wedding liturgy. The wedding feast of the Lamb refers to the union of Christ and his bride, the Church. It symbolizes the joyful occasion of the beginning of Christ's reign through the Church. Just as this wedding feast is symbolic, so the celebration of the Marriage of man and woman is also symbolic. The celebration of the rite of Marriage within the wedding liturgy symbolizes Christ's reign in your relationship with each other. Your love communicates the promise of love God has for all God's people.

Often the Book of Revelation is difficult to understand because of its symbolic language and references to the end times. For the most part, the vision in this reading is straightforward. Those in heaven resound with songs of joy. The day is wondrous! Those in heaven attest to God's glory with an "Alleluia." The only time in the New Testament this word appears is in this passage. A voice proclaims words from an Old Testament psalm, Psalm 115:13. A loud chorus that sounds like rushing water or thunder is so exuberant it repeats the "Alleluia," and announces the Lord's reign. The wedding feast could not be more amazing!

Truly this reading portrays all that you want your wedding day to be. Make yourselves ready in the best way possible to celebrate this glorious occasion. Think carefully about what you will wear. Know that your garment, like the one in the reading, reflects your holiness. Your baptismal garment is a gift from God that shows forth God's forgiving love. It is clean and bright, a free gift of grace from God in Jesus Christ. Your call is to keep it clean through your righteous deeds.

The victory song that is this reading concludes with one of seven beatitudes or blessings in the Book of Revelation. This beatitude speaks about those whom God calls to the Lamb's wedding feast. God calls you. God invites you as a couple. You have invited guests to witness to your Marriage on the joyful occasion of your wedding day. Choose music for the liturgy that resounds with an "Alleluia!" Hear the guests and you, as a couple, announce "Alleluia," for your love reveals the Lord's victory of love! Blessed indeed are you for your life continues as one great act of praise to God, who offers salvation to all who believe.

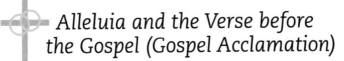

Alleluia and the Verse before the Gospel (Gospel Acclamation)

*Following the Second Reading, there is a period of silence. Then all stand for the Acclamation before the Gospel. This acclamation is usually Alleluia and is always sung by the assembly. A verse, sung by a choir or cantor, follows the acclamation, after which all repeat the sung refrain. This is often referred to as the Gospel Acclamation. In this section, you will find five options (**GA–1** to **GA–5**) from which to select as the verse.*

This is one of the shortest parts of the liturgy, but it is an important one, because we greet the Lord in song who is about to be present in the proclamation of the Gospel. The very word Alleluia is a profession of faith: in Hebrew, Alleluia means "praise God." Even in Lent, when we "fast" from singing the Alleluia, we substitute another acclamation that expresses much the same thing: "Glory and praise to you, Lord Jesus Christ!" or "Sing joyfully to God our strength," among other options, which your music director will help you choose.

Talk about the five options as a couple. Which of these acclamations speaks most directly to your own love story, your relationship with each other and with God?

*Be sure to talk to the music minister at your parish about the Acclamation before the Gospel. Countless musical settings of the "Alleluia" (or alternative Lenten form) have been composed, so you will have several to choose from. Record your Gospel Acclamation selection on the form on **page 92** and give it to your priest or deacon.*

GA-1

May the LORD bless you from Zion,

he who made both heaven and earth.

—Psalm 134:3

GA-2

This verse may be used during Lent. The alternate acclamation for Lent may be, "Sing joyfully to God our strength" (Psalm 81:2).

God is love,

If God loved us, we also must love one another.

—cf. 1 John 4:16b, 12, 11

GA-3

Everyone who loves is begotten

of God and knows God.

—1 John 4:7b

GA-4

If we love one another, God remains in us

and his love is brought to perfection in us.

—1 John 4:12

GA-5

Whoever remains in love,

remains in God and God in him.

—1 John 4:16

The Gospel Readings

In this section, you will find ten selections from the Gospel accounts along with commentaries to help you contextualize the Gospel and understand how it relates to your Marriage. The readings are numbered as G–1, G–2, and so on.

The Gospel readings, from the first four books of the New Testament, have a special place in the life of the Church. When the Gospel is proclaimed, Christ himself speaks to us today as he did to the crowds who gathered to listen to him long ago. Thus, the Gospel is the high point of the Liturgy of the Word, and is always proclaimed by a deacon or priest.

The Gospel readings provided here come from all four Gospel accounts — Matthew, Mark, Luke, and John. All the Gospel readings for weddings have something in common: they are all about love. In the teachings of Jesus, the two great loves — human love and divine love — can never be separated.

*As a couple, read and pray with each of these passages and the commentary that accompanies them. You will need to select one Gospel reading. One reading for your wedding liturgy must be about Marriage. These readings have been marked with an asterisk. Which passages do you find most comforting as you prepare for Marriage? Which passages challenge you? In which of these readings do you hear Jesus speaking most directly to you at this time in your lives? You will notice some readings have a long form and a short form to choose from. The short form is in brackets. Record your Gospel Reading selection on the form on **page 92** and give it to your priest or deacon.*

G–1 *Rejoice and be glad, for your reward will be great in heaven.*

A reading from the holy Gospel according to Matthew   *5:1–12a*

When Jesus saw the crowds, he went up the mountain,
> and after he had sat down, his disciples came to him.

He began to teach them, saying:

> "Blessed are the poor in spirit,
>> for theirs is the Kingdom of heaven.
> Blessed are they who mourn,
>> for they will be comforted.
> Blessed are the meek,
>> for they will inherit the land.
> Blessed are they who hunger and thirst for righteousness,
>> for they will be satisfied.
> Blessed are the merciful,
>> for they will be shown mercy.
> Blessed are the clean of heart,
>> for they will see God.
> Blessed are the peacemakers,
>> for they will be called children of God.
> Blessed are they who are persecuted for the sake of righteousness,
>> for theirs is the Kingdom of heaven.
> Blessed are you when they insult you and persecute you
>> and utter every kind of evil against you falsely because of me.
> Rejoice and be glad,
>> for your reward will be great in heaven."

The Gospel of the Lord.

You might select this reading because . . .

The Beatitudes touch your heart and you see them as the way to live as Christ lived. • You seek to peacefully resolve your arguments and are known as peacemakers among your friends and family. • Your commitment to helping others has made evident that acting mercifully is important to you.

If you select this reading, you might also consider . . .

Sirach 26:1–4, 13–16 **(OT–8)** • Psalm 112:1bc–2, 3–4, 5–7a, 7bc–8, 9 **(RP–4)** • Revelation 19:1, 5–9a **(NT–14)**

Background of the Gospel

One of the joys of getting married is thinking about your new family, your life together as a couple in a new home, your new extended family of in-laws and of course the possibility that God might bless your Marriage with children. This reading from Matthew is the opening of Jesus' most important sermon in all of the Gospel accounts. The Beatitudes here begin the Sermon on the Mount and they are all about how we are to act as Christians in the world. More importantly for you now though, is that the Beatitudes show us how we might raise our children to also be followers of Christ in the world.

Matthew is the first Gospel in the New Testament and is often thought of as the most Jewish account left to us by Christ. Jesus was of course a Jew and his earliest disciples were all Jewish. One feature of life within the ancient Jewish communities was how strict they were in teaching their children how to be good Jews, both in the community and in their dealings with the outside world. This often involved what to eat (kosher foods) and what to wear (fringes on clothing), but more important was how to be a follower of God in the treatment of others.

What we read in the Gospel according to Matthew is the story of Jesus taking this basic idea of Judaism, how to be a follower of God in the treatment of others, and bringing it to all the people of the world. Here in this Gospel reading Jesus sees these people, the crowd, and knows he must teach them the ways of God. He goes up the mountain to begin his most famous sermon.

If you as a couple choose this reading it would be because you have a special interest in building your Marriage—and future family life with children—around listening to what Jesus teaches us about how to be his follower, and so a follower of God, in a sometimes difficult and chaotic world.

What stands out in the Sermon on the Mount is that Christians are to be poor in spirit, that is, we are to be humble as persons and open to the feelings and sensitivities of others. We are to be eager to do what is right and merciful to those who wrong us. We are to be pure of heart and seek peace with others and in the world. What one sees in the Sermon on the Mount is a certain sort of person: a Christian. It is what we are all called to be in Christ and, most important for you as you begin your new family, is how we are to teach our children to be followers of God in Christ.

G–2 *You are the light of the world.*

A reading from the holy Gospel according to Matthew   *5:13–16*

Jesus said to his disciples:
"You are the salt of the earth.
But if salt loses its taste, with what can it be seasoned?
It is no longer good for anything
     but to be thrown out and trampled underfoot.
You are the light of the world.
A city set on a mountain cannot be hidden.
Nor do they light a lamp and then put it under a bushel basket;
     it is set on a lamp stand,
     where it gives light to all in the house.
Just so, your light must shine before others,
     that they may see your good deeds
     and glorify your heavenly Father."

The Gospel of the Lord.

You might select this reading because . . .
You understand that your relationship can set an example of God's love and care. •
Your involvement in your faith is such that you have discussed the importance of
rearing your children in the faith. • As a couple, you have sought to be true to your
faith, no matter the costs.

If you select this reading, you might also consider . . .
Proverbs 31:10–13, 19–20, 30–31 **(OT–6)** • Psalm 34:2–3, 4–5, 6–7, 8–9
(RP–2) • Hebrews 13:1–4a, 5–6b **(NT–10)**

Background of the Gospel

At the beginning of the Sermon on the Mount Jesus teaches the disciples around him. The crowds are curious about this new rabbi named Jesus and how one is to be his follower and a follower of God in the everyday world of human affairs. In the reading offered to you here, Jesus teaches us that just being a good person among family and friends is not enough. The Christian life is meant to be a public witness. It is meant to change the world by being a Christian in everything one does and everywhere one finds herself or himself to be in world.

If you as a couple choose this reading you are making a statement about how you want to live out your Marriage in public as a Christian couple. It is not just that you would choose as a couple to attend church along with your children but that you choose now to be an outwardly Christian family. Other couples and other families, for example, would notice that your own attitude and actions at work and in school meetings with teachers reflect the teaching of Christ in the Gospel readings. They would also notice that your children have been taught about Christ and reflect his teaching in their play with others and at school.

To choose this reading is to make a bold statement about what you will be as a couple and as a new family. It means you have accepted the call to begin to turn other people's hearts and minds to the ways of God taught by Christ. It means you have chosen not to tone down your Christian faith in order to blend in with society. On the contrary, your family will constantly bring out its faith in attitude and actions, like setting a lamp on a lampstand, for all to see. Is this the kind of family you choose to be?

G-3 *A wise man built his house on rock.*

A reading from the holy Gospel according to Matthew

Long form: 7:21, 24–29
[Short form: 7:21, 24–25]

[Jesus said to his disciples:
"Not everyone who says to me, 'Lord, Lord,'
    will enter the Kingdom of heaven,
    but only the one who does the will of my Father in heaven.

"Everyone who listens to these words of mine and acts on them
    will be like a wise man who built his house on rock.
The rain fell, the floods came,
    and the winds blew and buffeted the house.
But it did not collapse;
    it had been set solidly on rock.]
And everyone who listens to these words of mine
    but does not act on them
    will be like a fool who built his house on sand.
The rain fell, the floods came,
    and the winds blew and buffeted the house.
And it collapsed and was completely ruined."

When Jesus finished these words,
    the crowds were astonished at his teaching,
    for he taught them as one having authority,
    and not as their scribes.

The Gospel of the Lord.

You might select this reading because . . .
Your relationship has been tried through the death of a parent, sibling, or close friend, and your reliance on God carried you through the hard times.• As a couple, you reach out to help others, perhaps you are on the social justice commission in the parish, volunteer for Habitat for Humanity, or have cooked for a family who has lost a loved one. • Your relationship deepened through your contribution to the community's effort to help others.

If you select this reading, you might also consider . . .
Tobit 7:6–14 (OT–4) • Psalm 103:1–2, 8 and 13, 17–18a (RP–3) •
Romans 12:1–2, 9–18 (NT–2)

Background of the Gospel

Jesus in Matthew so often says what is not expected: "Be as wise as serpents and innocent as doves" (Matthew 10:16). What does that mean? In this reading, Jesus states that "not everyone who says to me 'Lord, Lord' will enter the Kingdom of heaven." So people who cry out to Jesus as Lord—people who are obviously Christians and know Jesus to be the Lord—will not enter into the Kingdom of Heaven? It is not what we would expect. The Gospel forces us to dig deeper into what Jesus is teaching us in this reading.

The reading here is the conclusion to the Sermon on the Mount, the centerpiece of Jesus' teaching in Matthew and, even more, the centerpiece of Jesus' teaching in the whole of the New Testament. The focus of the Sermon on the Mount is on Christian action, the Greek word for "doing" (poieō) is featured throughout the Sermon. The Sermon in particular, and the Gospel according to Matthew as a whole, states clearly that the Christian life is based not only in what one believes but also in how one puts that belief into action. For example, it is only within the Gospel according to Matthew that we find out how we will be judged by Christ at the end of our lives: did we feed the hungry, give drink to the thirsty; did we welcome the stranger, clothe the naked and visit the sick (see Matthew 25:31–46)?

If you as a couple choose this reading you will be showing to those at your wedding that you believe your family life will include a call not just to Christian faith—to call Jesus Lord—but to put Christian faith into action. If you as a couple and as a new family see yourselves involved in the ministries of social justice at your church, involved with helping to stock food shelves and provide shelter for the homeless, then this is certainly the right Gospel for your wedding.

G-4 *What God has united, man must not separate.*

A reading from the holy Gospel according to Matthew   *19:3–6**

Some Pharisees approached Jesus, and tested him, saying,
   "Is it lawful for a man to divorce his wife for any cause whatever?"
He said in reply, "Have you not read that from the beginning
      the Creator *made them male and female* and said,
      For this reason a man shall leave his father and mother
      and be joined to his wife, and the two shall become one flesh?
So they are no longer two, but one flesh.
Therefore, what God has joined together,
   man must not separate."

The Gospel of the Lord.

You might select this reading because . . .
You feel that God has brought you together and that you are to act as Christ
to each other. • As a couple, you have discussed centering your family life on
commitment to what God calls you to. • In your relationship, you strive to mirror the
unity that Christ seeks to have with each of us.

If you select this reading, you might also consider . . .
Genesis 1:26–28, 31a **(OT–1)** • Psalm 128:1–2, 3, 4–5ac and 6a **(RP–5)** •
Ephesians 5:2a, 21–33 **(NT–7)**

Background of the Gospel

This Gospel passage from Matthew is one of the most famous and most difficult teachings of Jesus. Jesus' teaching about Marriage and divorce can also be found in the Gospel accounts of Mark (10:2–12) and Luke (16:18), as well as the New Testament letters of Paul (1 Corinthians 7:10–11). In each case the emphasis of the teaching is on the permanence of Marriage. In our society today, with divorce rates as high as they are, we in the Church should try to understand this teaching from both its ancient Jewish and early Christian roots.

In this Gospel reading, the Pharisees approach Jesus with a precise question: "Is it lawful for a man to divorce his wife for any cause whatever?" What stands out in this question is its presumption: only a man can divorce his wife (a woman cannot divorce her husband) and it can be done without cause. In ancient Jewish practice a husband simply handed his wife a certificate of divorce and, voila!, there was a divorce. In the ancient world this would have meant that many women, who were not routinely educated or trained for work outside the home, would have been left destitute within Jewish society. As a result we can see that Jesus' teaching here actually protects the interests and welfare of women by not allowing divorce within the newly formed Christian communities.

More important, however, is to understand why Jesus taught us that Marriage is permanent. And this might help you to choose this Gospel for your own wedding. Jesus reveals to us who we are as a Christian community. To be "in Christ" from our Baptism is be part of the Resurrection of Christ, a return to what we were meant to be from the very beginning of God's creation: men and women who love each other, are open to new life, and care for others along with all of creation. Whenever we enter a sacrament like Baptism or the Eucharist or Marriage we are entering into that original condition of what God meant for us to be. To choose this Gospel for your wedding is to say that you will—with your Marriage vows—always attempt to be in your Marriage and family life part of what God has wanted for us from the beginning.

G–5 *This is the greatest and the first commandment. The second is like it.*

A reading from the holy Gospel according to Matthew   *22:35–40*

One of the Pharisees, a scholar of the law, tested Jesus by asking,
   "Teacher, which commandment in the law is the greatest?"
He said to him,
   "You shall love the Lord, your God,
   with all your heart,
   with all your soul,
   and with all your mind.
This is the greatest and first commandment.
The second is like it:
   You shall love your neighbor as yourself.
The whole law and the prophets depend on these two commandments."

The Gospel of the Lord.

You might select this reading because . . .
As a couple, you pray together and seek ways to spread God's love through charitable work. • You plan to continue to make room in your lives for community and parish work that reaches out to others. • Your relationship has deepened through your volunteer work in a shelter, a nursing home, or a tutoring center.

If you select this reading, you might also consider . . .
Jeremiah 31:31–32a, 33–34a **(OT–9)** • Psalm 145:8–9, 10 and 15, 17–18 **(RP–6)** • 1 Corinthians 12:31—13:8a **(NT–5)**

Background of the Gospel

In the Gospel according to Matthew, the Pharisees always seem to be challenging Jesus. Over many centuries of Christians reading about their arguments with Jesus they have, in simple terms, gotten a bad rap. In fact, many people use the terms Pharisee or Pharisaic to mean someone is too picky about nonessentials or interested in trivial matters rather than issues that really count. Even within the Gospel according to Matthew this characterization of the ancient Jewish Pharisees is not fair. The Pharisees were primarily interested in establishing the social norms and practices of ancient Judaism as the Jewish religion spread out from the ancient land of Israel to new lands and new cultures. In fact, over time, the ways of being Jewish established by the Pharisees became our modern day understanding of the Jewish religion.

As Christianity itself spread in ancient Israel to the lands of the Roman Empire, the new religion met, as you might expect, Jewish communities already heavily influenced by the teachings of the Pharisees about how to be Jewish. In these early days Christians did not think of themselves as Christians but as Jews who followed the teachings of the Rabbi Jesus, the Messiah and Son of God. Therefore, great conflict developed between the Jews who followed Jesus and the Jews who followed the Pharisees. It is this conflict that is featured prominently in the pages of Matthew's account of the Gospel.

If you as a couple choose this Gospel for your wedding you would be making a statement about the commandments that would be at the heart of your new family life. To say that your new family will love God above all else means that you will make choices about how you live that are often countercultural. Will your family put prayer and the love of God above the desire for more income and a larger house? To say that you will love your neighbor as yourself means that you will put others' needs on par with your own, that you will respond in love to family, friends, and strangers when they need your attention and even part of your treasure. If this is the kind of family you desire to build by getting married, then this Gospel will fit nicely at your wedding.

G-6 *They are no longer two, but one flesh.*

A reading from the holy Gospel according to Mark   *10:6–9**

Jesus said:
"From the beginning of creation,
  God made them male and female.
For this reason a man shall leave his father and mother
    and be joined to his wife,
    and the two shall become one flesh.
So they are no longer two but one flesh.
Therefore what God has joined together,
    no human being must separate."

The Gospel of the Lord.

You might select this reading because . . .
In Marriage, you see a commitment to manifest the love that God has given you. •
You give God thanks for bringing you together and will rely on God to keep you
as one. • As a couple, you see the Sacrament of Matrimony as a way the Church
concretizes the goodness God has given us in each other.

If you select this reading, you might also consider . . .
Genesis 2:18–24 **(OT–2)** • Psalm 33:12 and 18, 20–21, 22 **(RP-1)** •
1 Corinthians 6:13c–15a, 17–20 **(NT–4)**

Background of the Gospel

This short reading from Mark is powerful! "From the beginning of creation *God made them male and female.*" At the heart of the Church's understanding of Marriage is the complimentary difference in the two biological sexes. This difference allows each of us, as male or female, to understand and experience the world in unique ways and also to know that as a male or a female we are limited in our understanding. Each of the sexes needs the other to know what it means to be fully human. From this encounter, male and female, we get new life: "*and the two shall become one flesh.*" From a Christian perspective taught to us by Christ in the Gospel this encounter is not just about sexual union, as important as that is to married life. Rather, this encounter is to enter deeply into the amazing personal mystery of your husband or your wife, as male or female, over an entire lifetime of Marriage. It is in exploring that mystery of the other person that we find out more about ourselves, that is, why God made humans male and female to begin with.

If you as a couple choose this Gospel it will be because you are deeply fascinated by this mystery of what makes us human. You will choose this Gospel because you celebrate just how different you are as male and female and how committed you are to engaging deeply the mystery, the sexual difference, that is at the core of the person you are marrying. In doing so the two of you will "*become one flesh,*" that is, you will begin to understand more completely what it means to be human. In this way you will put Christ, the fullness of what it means to be human, at the center of your Marriage.

The Church teaches us that Marriage is a sacrament, that is, as a sacrament, Marriage physically makes visible to all of us the Resurrected Christ. This Gospel passage from Mark tells us why this is so. When male and female become one flesh, one body, they show by both their intimate union and their love for each other in public, the resurrected Body of Christ. In short, in the Sacrament of Matrimony the two, male and female, have become one body, the Body of Christ.

G–7 *Jesus did this as the beginning of his signs in Cana in Galilee.*

A reading from the holy Gospel according to John   *2:1–11**

There was a wedding in Cana in Galilee,
>and the mother of Jesus was there.

Jesus and his disciples were also invited to the wedding.

When the wine ran short,
>the mother of Jesus said to him,
>"They have no wine."

And Jesus said to her,
>"Woman, how does your concern affect me? My hour has not yet come."

His mother said to the servers,
>"Do whatever he tells you."

Now there were six stone water jars there for Jewish ceremonial washings,
>each holding twenty to thirty gallons.

Jesus told them,
>"Fill the jars with water."

So they filled them up to the brim.

Then he told them,
>"Draw some out now and take it to the headwaiter."

So they took it.

And when the headwaiter tasted the water that had become wine,
>without knowing where it came from
>(although the servants who had drawn the water knew),
>the headwaiter called the bridegroom and said to him,
>"Everyone serves good wine first,
>and then when people have drunk freely, an inferior one;
>but you have kept the good wine until now."

Jesus did this as the beginning of his signs in Cana in Galilee
>and so revealed his glory,
>and his disciples began to believe in him.

The Gospel of the Lord.

You might select this reading because . . .
You understand the Eucharist as God's pouring out an abundance of love.• As a couple, you know that you seek to reveal God's glory in the kindnesses you show each other and those you encounter. • Your relationship is connected to your faith and, as disciples of Christ, you strive to share God's abundant joy at work, school, and in the community.

If you select this reading, you might also consider . . .
Tobit 7:6–14 (**OT–4**) • Psalm 34:2–3, 4–5, 6–7, 8–9 (**RP–2**) •
Revelation 19:1, 5–9a (**NT–14**)

Background of the Gospel

This story from John is by far the most widely read Gospel at Catholic weddings. There is a good reason for this. It is the only story of a wedding in all of the Gospel accounts. So naturally couples like to read the story of Jesus attending a wedding at their own wedding! This makes sense, but if you as a couple want to choose this reading for your wedding you should know that there is far more to this story than just a wedding attended by Jesus, his mother, and his disciples.

First, the story centers on the fact that the wedding party was running short on wine. How plausible is this? Would those preparing the wedding not have made sure there was enough wine for all of the guests? Why are there exactly six very large stone water jars present and why are they empty? Why does Jesus ask to have each of them filled to the brim with twenty to thirty gallons of water? Who is the anonymous bridegroom who is given credit by the headwaiter for saving the best wine for last?

The story of the wedding in John's account of the Gospel is really a story about the Eucharist. It is about Jesus Christ who comes to us bringing the new wine of his blood just at the time when we most need it. It is about the abundance that God provides for us as we realize that the Kingdom of God, the new seven-day creation, is breaking into our world as we imitate Christ in our love for strangers, the poor and those in need. Honestly, think about how much wine is made present at this wedding with each jar holding just twenty gallons: that is 120 gallons of wine for one wedding! And the bridegroom who saves the best wine for last? Is that not Jesus Christ who comes to marry his Church and give himself to it in the wine of the Eucharist?

It surely makes sense for you as a couple to choose this story of a wedding for your own wedding, especially for a wedding celebrated within a Mass. Remember though that the story of abundance and celebration, the gallons of water made into wine, is the story of God's love for us in the sacrifice of Christ's Blood on the Cross (John 19:34). As the Apostle Paul says, we were bought for a price (1 Corinthians 7:23), so let us be thankful, and yes, celebrate, that the price has been paid.

G-8 *Remain in my love.*

A reading from the holy Gospel according to John   *15:9–12*

Jesus said to his disciples:
"As the Father loves me, so I also love you.
Remain in my love.
If you keep my commandments, you will remain in my love,
    just as I have kept my Father's commandments
    and remain in his love.

"I have told you this so that my joy might be in you
    and your joy might be complete.
This is my commandment: love one another as I love you."

The Gospel of the Lord.

You might select this reading because . . .
As a couple, you are nourished by praying together, and through prayer, seek to
remain in God's love. • You are both aware that love involves sacrifice, and you are
willing to endure those struggles for the joy in your relationship. • You have seen
each other through difficult times and know that love is not easy.

If you select this reading, you might also consider . . .
Song of Songs 2:8–10, 14, 16a; 8:6–7a **(OT–7)** • Psalm 145:8–9, 10 and 15,
17–18 **(RP–6)** • 1 John 3:18–24 **(NT–12)**

Background of the Gospel

At the very end of chapter 14 in John's account, the Last Supper is over. Jesus commands the disciples to "Get up, let us go" (John 14:31). At this point the story in John is interrupted by Jesus' very long speech, a speech that lasts for four chapters! At the end of the speech Jesus leads his disciples into the Garden at Gethsemane. The Gospel reading here comes toward the beginning of this long speech and it centers on the love Jesus has for his disciples—and all of us—just at the moment when he is about to be betrayed (Judas) and denied (Peter) by these very disciples. And herein lies the message of this reading.

In any Marriage there are going to be times when you hurt the one that you love the most, whether by accident or design. It is the great mystery of Marriage that when two people become as close as two people can be with each other, when two people can love each other more than they ever thought possible, that they can end up fighting and hurting their cherished partner. How are we to understand that? More importantly, what are we to do knowing this is the inevitable reality of Marriage?

The answer lies in the Gospel reading here and it is the reason that you as a couple might choose this Gospel passage for your wedding. When Jesus says that he loves his disciples he knows they will eventually hurt him, yet he does not hesitate to declare his love for them. When he tells his disciples to love one another as Jesus loves them, he is telling them to love one another despite the fact that they will inevitably hurt each other and Jesus. The love that Jesus calls for here is not some pie in the sky love, a love filled with flowers and lace of a wedding day, but love that lasts through the pain and hurts of a long and beautiful Marriage. If you as a couple are ready for that long journey of Marriage, ready to love your spouse in the shadow of the pain she or he inevitably will cause you, whether by intention or accident, then yes, choose this reading from John.

G-9 *This is my commandment: love one another.*

A reading from the holy Gospel according to John *15:12–16*

Jesus said to his disciples:
"This is my commandment: love one another as I love you.
No one has greater love than this,
    to lay down one's life for one's friends.
You are my friends if you do what I command you.
I no longer call you slaves,
    because a slave does not know what his master is doing.
I have called you friends,
    because I have told you everything I have heard from my Father.
It was not you who chose me, but I who chose you
    and appointed you to go and bear fruit that will remain,
    so that whatever you ask the Father in my name he may give you."

The Gospel of the Lord.

You might select this reading because . . .
As a couple, you have sought friendship with Christ through prayer together and
retreats. • You value your friendship with each other as much as your love for each
other. • The trust that you have for one another is the trust of good and faithful
friends and you seek to increase that friendship with Marriage.

If you select this reading, you might also consider . . .
Genesis 24:48–51, 58–67 **(OT–3)** • Psalm 112:1bc–2, 3–4, 5–7a, 7bc–8, 9b **(RP–4)** •
Romans 15:1b–3a, 5–7, 13 **(NT–3)**

Background of the Gospel

"You are my friends if you do what I command you" (John 15:14). So what does Jesus command? "Love one another as I love you" (John 15:12). How does Jesus love? He has laid "down his life for his friends" (John 15:13). What does this reading have to do with a wedding?

This Gospel reading has primarily to do with friendship. Friendship, even more than love, is the anchor for a good and lasting Marriage. Ask any married couple who have been married for a long time and they will tell you this. Why? Because love so often has to do with sacrifice, your willingness to be so overwhelmed by your feelings for your spouse that you will do anything, even sacrifice your sense of self, to make that person happy. And when you lose yourselves within Marriage there is no one there for your partner to love. It is a hard lesson that can take couples years to learn. When there are two strong persons in a Marriage there will be tension, and out of that tension will come both friendship and great passionate love.

This is why in the Gospel according to John, Jesus begins with friendship and then moves to love. Friendship is based on mutual respect and admiration. It is based on seeing the good qualities in the other person and the sheer enjoyment of that person's company. In true friendship you know you can be yourself without pretense because the other person knows you so well. And in the freedom to be your true self with another person you come to grow and understand yourself better than you ever have before.

If you as a couple choose this Gospel reading it may be because you are captured by this logic of friendship and love. In this reading, Jesus says that in our love for each other we become friends with him. We can be our true selves with Christ because he knows us so well. And as we grow as persons from our friendship with Christ, we offer more to our partner in Marriage. And as we love our spouse more and more, as we give our life to that person, we still find friendship within the passion of Marriage.

G–10 *That they may be brought to perfection as one.*

A reading from the holy Gospel according to John

Long Form: 17:20–26
[Short Form: 17:20–23]

[Jesus raised his eyes to heaven and said:
"I pray not only for my disciples,
> but also for those who will believe in me through their word,
> so that they may all be one,
> as you, Father, are in me and I in you,
> that they also may be in us,
> that the world may believe that you sent me.
And I have given them glory you gave me,
> so that they may be one, as we are one,
> I in them and you in me,
> that they may be brought to perfection as one,
> that the world may know that you sent me,
> and that you loved them even as you loved me.]
Father, they are your gift to me.
I wish that where I am they also may be with me,
> that they may see my glory that you gave me,
> because you loved me before the foundation of the world.
Righteous Father, the world also does not know you,
> but I know you, and they know that you sent me.
I made known to them your name and I will make it known,
> that the love with which you loved me
> may be in them and I in them."

The Gospel of the Lord.

You might select this reading because . . .
You attribute your love to God and seek closeness to each other through your relationship with him. • As a couple, you rejoice in the closeness that you share with family and friends. • Your relationship seems to be a gift from God, and you share that gift through loving others.

If you select this reading, you might also consider . . .
Jeremiah 31:31–32a, 33–34a **(OT–9)** • Psalm 33:12 and 18, 20–21, 22 **(RP–1)** • 1 John 4:7–12 **(NT–13)**

Background of the Gospel

This Gospel reading from John is about the community at your wedding. It is about the Church that Christ gave to us—the Church within which you are about to be married. You as a couple might choose this reading if you have a strong sense that your Marriage is as much about belonging to your Church community, family, and friends as it is about you two as an isolated couple.

The family you are about to create (you and your spouse are a new family, children add to that family) is called the domestic Church—for good reason. The love and harmony between you and your spouse will at first be a witness for Christ to your friends, neighbors, and coworkers, and then, should it be God's will, the first witness for Christ that your children will experience. All of these people, but especially your children, will come to know that Christ is real because Christ is real in the unity and joy of your Marriage. It will be your children's first encounter with sacrament, the reality of Christ in our world.

The gathered assembly at your wedding will include members of the Church. Usually, there are also a fair number of nonpracticing Catholics and people of other faiths or of no faith. For active Catholics, a wedding is an occasion to share your happiness and to welcome you into the greater unity of married Christians, who are experiencing in their lives the love and unity that you are pledging on the day of your Marriage. The love and unity of married Christians gives witness to the love and unity of Christ and his Church. It is this symbolism that has led the Church to see Marriage as a sacrament—a way of making the faithful love of Christ present in our world and a way for God's grace to strengthen the couple to live like Jesus "in good times and in bad, / in sickness and in health, / . . . all the days of [your] life" (*The Order of Celebrating Matrimony*, 62).

At your wedding, God's love and joy will flood into the assembly through your witness as a couple. And God's love and joy will flood into you as a couple through the witness of unity in the assembly. It will be a happy and glorious day as you share and model for others the love of Christ present in our world. Reason enough to choose this Gospel for the celebration.

The Celebration of Matrimony

In this section you will find options for the prayers and other texts that accompany the key moments in the Celebration of Matrimony: the questions before the consent, the consent (C–1 to C–4), the reception of the consent (RC–1 and RC–2), the blessing and giving of rings (BR–1 to BR–3), the Prayer of the Faithful (page 86), and the Nuptial Blessing (NB–1 to NB–3).

The Celebration of Matrimony always takes place after the homily, whether or not Mass is celebrated. The Matrimony ritual is the heart of the celebration. It is at this time in the ritual that you will become husband and wife. You will want to spend time discussing the options provided in this resource as a couple. What speaks most powerfully to you and the life you are preparing to live together? What reflects your love for each other and your love for God? Record your selections on the form on page 92 and give it to your priest or deacon.

Questions before the Consent

When exchanging consent, or your vows, you agree to give yourselves to each other in Matrimony. The priest or deacon will ask you to respond seperately to the following questions. The question regarding children may be omitted if you are an older couple. It is included below so that you are aware of the questions and how to respond before your ceremony.

N. and **N.**, have you come here to enter into Marriage
without coercion,
freely and wholeheartedly?
R. I have.

Are you prepared, as you follow the path of Marriage,
to love and honor each other
for as long as you both shall live?
R. I am.

Are you prepared to accept children lovingly from God
and to bring them up
according to the law of Christ and his Church?
R. I am.

The Consent

The consent is what makes the Marriage—the moment where you become husband and wife. Joining your right hands you promise to be a sign of Christ's love for all of your lives. Select from one of the options presented below. Option **C–1** or **C–2** may be memorized or repeated after the presider. Each of you will recite to each other the text you've chosen. Or, if you choose either **C–3** or **C–4**, you may respond with "I do" to a series of questions.

C–1 *Option 1, Recited*
I, **N.**, take you, **N.**, to be my
    wife [/husband].
I promise to be faithful to you,
in good times and in bad,
in sickness and in health,
to love you and to honor you
all the days of my life.

C–2 *Option 2, Recited*
I, **N.**, take you, **N.**, for my
    lawful wife [/husband],
to have and to hold,
    from this day forward,
for better, for worse,
for richer, for poorer,
in sickness and in health,
to love and to cherish,
until death do us part.

C–3 *Option 3, Questions*
N., do you take **N.**, to be your
    wife [/husband]?
Do you promise to be faithful
    to her [/him]
in good times and in bad,
in sickness and in health,
to love her and to honor her [/him]
all the days of your life?

R: I do.

C–4 *Option 4, Questions*
N., do you take **N.**, for your lawful
    wife [/husband],
to have and to hold,
    from this day forward,
for better, for worse,
for richer, for poorer,
in sickness and in health,
to love and to cherish,
until death do you part?

R: I do.

The Reception of the Consent

Next, the priest or deacon verifies that you have declared your consent before God. Select one of the following two options. After the reception of the consent the priest will say, "Let us bless the Lord." All reply, "Thanks be to God."

RC-1

May the Lord in his kindness
    strengthen the consent
you have declared before the Church,
and graciously bring to fulfillment his
    blessing within you.
What God joins together,
    let no one put asunder.

RC-2

May the God of Abraham, the God
    of Isaac, the God of Jacob,
the God who joined together
    our first parents in paradise,
strengthen and bless in Christ
the consent you have declared
    before the Church,
so that what God joins together, no one
    may put asunder.

The Blessing of Rings

The blessing and giving of rings is the primary sign of unity within the wedding ceremony. The rings are blessed to be a sign and reminder of your love as a couple. Select one of the three options provided below.

BR-1 *Option 1*

May the Lord bless ✝ these rings,
which you will give to each other
as a sign of love and fidelity.
R. Amen.

BR-3 *Option 3*

Bless ✝ and sanctify your servants
in their love, O Lord,
and let these rings,
    a sign of their faithfulness,
remind them of their love
    for one another.
Through Christ our Lord.
R. Amen.

BR-2 *Option 2*

Bless, O Lord, these rings,
which we bless ✝ in your name,
so that those who wear them
may remain entirely
    faithful to each other,
abide in peace and in your will,
and live always in mutual charity.
Through Christ our Lord.
R. Amen.

The Giving of Rings

There is only one option for the giving of rings. During the wedding ceremony, you will say the following text to each other. The text in brackets may be omitted if the one saying it is not baptized.

N., receive this ring
as a sign of my love and fidelity.
[In the name of the Father, and of the Son,
and of the Holy Spirit.]

The Prayer of the Faithful

The Prayer of the Faithful (also called the Universal Prayer), follows the blessing and giving of rings. This prayer presents a series of petitions for the needs of the Church, the world, the afflicted, and the local community. At a wedding, petitions may be included for the needs of the couple. This prayer is a good reminder that we do not pray simply for ourselves at a supremely happy moment—we pause and remember in prayer the world of which we are a part, and for which we have a responsibility as Christian believers. You may use these sample petitions at your own wedding or use these samples as a guide for writing your own. Your parish priest, deacon, or music and liturgy director will also be able to help you.

Parts of the prayer are bold. Directions for writing the prayer are italic. Sample prayers are centered text.

Introduction

Notice that this is not a prayer, addressed to God, but an invitation to prayer addressed to all present. It is read by the priest or deacon presiding at the wedding liturgy.

> As we pray to the Lord for [*name of the bride*]
> and [*name of the groom*] on their wedding day,
> let us also remember the needs of the Church and the world.

Petitions

The petitions always follow the same pattern: we pray for the Church, the world, the afflicted, and the local community. Additional petitions may be added. These are read by a deacon or reader, usually a family member or friend, or sung by a cantor.

For the Church:

> For Christians everywhere,
> that the world may see our love for one another and come to believe,
> we pray to the Lord:

For the world:

> For peace among nations,
> that there may be an end to the violence that divides us,
> we pray to the Lord:

For the oppressed:

> For all who are marginalized or forgotten by our society,
> and for all to love and pray for them,
> that God will use us to raise them up,
> we pray to the Lord:

For the local community:

> For all who are part of our lives,
> our parents, friends, and companions along the way,
> and for all who have helped to bring us to this day,
> we pray to the Lord:

Additional petitions:

> For [*name of the bride*] and [*name of the groom*],
> that the love they pledge to each other today may bring
> light and joy into their lives and the lives of others,
> we pray to the Lord:

> For all our beloved dead,
> especially [*insert the names of those who have died*],
> we pray to the Lord:

Response of the Assembly

The response to each petition by those attending your ceremony is an important part of the prayer. So that your assembly can participate better, it's best if you use a response that most will know, such as: **Lord, hear our prayer**.

Concluding Prayer

The presiding priest or deacon will conclude the Prayer of the Faithful with a short prayer. A simple way to construct this prayer is to use this format, **You**, **Who**, **Do**, **Through**. *Address the prayer to God, the Father (***You***) and note that he acts in a particular way (***Who***). Indicate something the Father or Son has done or will do for us (***Do***) and conclude with the ending found in the example below (***Through***). The concluding prayer is omitted if your wedding takes place without Mass. Instead, the Nuptial Blessing is prayed (see* **page 88**).

YOU: God of love,

WHO: you have taught us that all things are passing
 in this changing world,
 all except love.

DO: Help us to seek your love above all things,
 and to love all people as you love them.

THROUGH: Through Christ our Lord.

 Amen.

The Nuptial Blessing

The Nuptial Blessing is an important part of the wedding liturgy. This long, rich prayer invokes the blessing of God—Father, Son, and Holy Spirit—on the newly married couple, and prays that they may remain united in love throughout their lives, and be united again in the Kingdom of Heaven. The blessing also asks that the couple be blessed with children and be given strength to be good parents (although this section could be omitted if you are an older couple). As you select the prayer for your wedding, read each prayer carefully. What do the prayers say about Marriage? How do the prayers express your commitment to each other and your Christian faith? If one of you is not baptized, you should select option four **(NB–4)**. The blessing may be sung. Consult with your music director and presider about this option.

NB–1 Option 1

O God, who by your mighty power
created all things out of nothing,
and, when you had set in place
the beginnings of the universe,
formed man and woman in your own image,
making the woman an inseparable helpmate to the man,
that they might no longer be two, but one flesh,
and taught that what you were pleased to make one
must never be divided;

O God, who consecrated the bond of Marriage
by so great a mystery
that in the wedding covenant you foreshadowed
the Sacrament of Christ and his Church;

O God, by whom woman is joined to man
and the companionship they had in the beginning
is endowed with the one blessing
not forfeited by original sin
nor washed away by the flood.

Look now with favor on these your servants,
joined together in Marriage,
who ask to be strengthened by your blessing.
Send down on them the grace of the Holy Spirit
and pour your love into their hearts,
that they may remain faithful in the Marriage covenant.

May the grace of love and peace
abide in your daughter **N.**,
and let her always follow the example of those holy women
whose praises are sung in the Scriptures.

May her husband entrust his heart to her,
so that, acknowledging her as his equal
and his joint heir to the life of grace,
he may show her due honor
and cherish her always
with the love that Christ has for his Church.

And now, Lord, we implore you:
may these your servants
hold fast to the faith and keep your commandments;
made one in the flesh,
may they be blameless in all they do;
and with the strength that comes from the Gospel,
may they bear true witness to Christ before all;
(may they be blessed with children,
and prove themselves virtuous parents,
who live to see their children's children).

And grant that,
reaching at last together the fullness of years
for which they hope,
they may come to the life of the blessed
in the Kingdom of Heaven.
Through Christ our Lord.
R. Amen.

NB-2 *Option 2*

Holy Father,
who formed man in your own image,
male and female you created them,
so that as husband and wife, united in body and heart,
they might fulfill their calling in the world;

O God, who, to reveal the great design you formed in your love,
willed that the love of spouses for each other
should foreshadow the covenant you graciously made with
          your people,
so that, by fulfillment of the sacramental sign,
the mystical marriage of Christ with his Church
might become manifest
in the union of husband and wife among your faithful;

Graciously stretch out your right hand
over these your servants (**N.** and **N.**), we pray,
and pour into their hearts the power of the Holy Spirit.

Grant, O Lord,
that, as they enter upon this sacramental union,
they may share with one another the gifts of your love
and, by being for each other a sign of your presence,
become one heart and one mind.

May they also sustain, O Lord, by their deeds
the home they are forming
(and prepare their children
to become members of your heavenly household
by raising them in the way of the Gospel).

Graciously crown with your blessings your daughter **N.**,
so that, by being a good wife (and mother),
she may bring warmth to her home with a love that is pure
and adorn it with welcoming graciousness.

Bestow a heavenly blessing also, O Lord,
on **N.**, your servant,
that he may be a worthy, good and
faithful husband (and a provident father).

Grant, holy Father, that, desiring to approach your table
as a couple joined in Marriage in your presence,
they may one day have the joy
of taking part in your great banquet in heaven.
Through Christ our Lord.
R. Amen.

NB–3 Option 3

Holy Father, maker of the whole world,
who created man and woman in your own image
and willed that their union be crowned with your blessing,
we humbly beseech you for these your servants,
who are joined today in the Sacrament of Matrimony.

May your abundant blessing, Lord,
come down upon this bride, **N.**,
and upon **N.**, her companion for life,
and may the power of your Holy Spirit
set their hearts aflame from on high,
so that, living out together the gift of Matrimony,
they may (adorn their family with children
and) enrich the Church.

In happiness may they praise you, O Lord,
in sorrow may they seek you out;
may they have the joy of your presence
to assist them in their toil,
and know that you are near
to comfort them in their need;
let them pray to you in the holy assembly
and bear witness to you in the world,
and after a happy old age,
together with the circle of friends that surrounds them,
may they come to the Kingdom of Heaven.
Through Christ our Lord.
R. Amen.

NB–4 Option 4

Select this option if one of you is not baptized.
Holy Father, maker of the whole world,
who created man and woman in your own image
and willed that their union be crowned with your blessing,
we humbly beseech you for these your servants,
who are joined today in the Marriage covenant.
May your abundant blessing, Lord,
come down upon this bride, **N.**,
and upon **N.**, her companion for life,
and may the power of your Holy Spirit
set their hearts aflame from on high,
so that, living out together the gift of Matrimony,
they may be known for the integrity of their conduct
(and be recognized as virtuous parents).

In happiness may they praise you, O Lord,
in sorrow may they seek you out;
may they have the joy of your presence
to assist them in their toil,
and know that you are near
to comfort them in their need;
and after a happy old age,
together with the circle of friends that surrounds them,
may they come to the Kingdom of Heaven.
Through Christ our Lord.
R. Amen.

UNITED IN CHRIST *Preparing the Liturgy of the Word at Catholic Weddings*

BRIDE: _____ GROOM: _____

DATE OF WEDDING: _____ TIME OF WEDDING: _____

CHURCH: _____

Selection Form

After you have selected the Scripture readings and the prayers you would like to use at your wedding, you will need to record them on this form and give it the priest or deacon who is presiding at your wedding. You may use this page or download an editable PDF from this website: www.ltp.org/UIC_selection_form.

The Readings

OLD TESTAMENT READING	OT–1 TO OT–9	PAGES 1–19
RESPONSORIAL PSALM	RP–2 TO RP–7	PAGES 21–28
NEW TESTAMENT READING	NT–1 TO NT–14	PAGES 29–57
GOSPEL ACCLAMATION	GA–1 TO GA–5	PAGES 59–60
GOSPEL READING	G–1 TO G–10	PAGES 61–81

The Celebration of Matrimony

THE CONSENT	C–1 TO C–4	PAGE 84
RECEPTION OF CONSENT	RC–1 TO RC–2	PAGE 85
BLESSING OF RINGS	BR–1 TO BR–3	PAGE 85
NUPTIAL BLESSING	NB–1 TO NB–4	PAGES 88–91

The Prayer of the Faithful

Prior to the wedding, be sure to e-mail your presider a copy of the petitions that you have written.